W9-AAQ-595

SEASONS IN THE HOME

WINTER

CREATIVE
HOME
ARTS
—CLUB—

CREATIVE HOME ARTS LIBRARY™

WIN

CREATIVE HOME ARTS CLUB
MINNETONKA, MINNESOTA

CREDITS

SEASONS IN THE HOME
WINTER

Printed in 2006.

Tom Carpenter
Creative Director

Heather Koshiol
Managing Editor

Jennifer Weaverling
Senior Book Development Coordinator

Jenya Prosmitsky
Book Design & Production

3 4 5 6 7 8 / 08 07 06 05
ISBN 1-58159-207-8
© 2004 Creative Home Arts Club

Creative Home Arts Club
12301 Whitewater Drive
Minnetonka, Minnesota 55343
www.creativehomeartsclub.com

Contributing Writers

Walter Chandoha
Mary Evans
Jana Freiband
Lisa Golden Schroeder
Zoe Graul
Doreen Howard
Patsy Jamieson
Sue Jorgensen
Janel Leatherman
Michelle Leise
Colleen Miner
Cheryl Natt
Yula Nelson
Beatrice Ojakangas
John Schumacher
Ruth Zavitz

Contributing Photographers

Bill Lindner Photography
Mark Macemon
Tad Ware & Company, Inc.

Additional Photography

David Cavagnaro
Walter Chandoha
Crandall & Crandall
Alan and Linda Detrick
Derek Fell
Harry Haralambou
Michael Hendrickson
Jerry Pavia
Amy Sumner
Darrel Trout

Special thanks to: Mike Billstein, Terry Casey, Janice Cauley and Nadine Trimble.

Contents

SEASONS IN THE HOME

WINTER

INTRODUCTION

There are plenty of reasons to love winter. Yes, cool, cold or downright frigid winds may blow. And rain, snow flurries or a full-fledge blizzard may fall. But those are just good reasons to cozy up at home, without guilt about being indoors.

Winter is also a wonderful time to make your home an even more beautiful and comfortable place.

Long evenings offer the free time you need to complete seasonal and other important decorating projects.

Brisk afternoons were made for crafting at the kitchen table — perhaps with friends, perhaps with children or grandchildren, or maybe in some much-deserved quiet time by yourself.

Winter was made for cooking too. What better time to make hot and satisfying soups? Dinners that could be classified as "comfort food" but are still good for you? Warm desserts fresh from the oven? The season offers you a little more time to cook for yourself, family and friends … and really enjoy the process.

Yes, winter is for cocooning. But it's also the perfect time for entertaining — for the holidays, for a ball game, for a dinner party, or "just because!"

Those are the kinds of ideas you'll find in *Seasons in the Home — Winter*. These project- and picture-filled pages will keep you busy all winter long, and for many winters to come, as you craft, decorate, cook (and even garden) your way to an even more inviting home.

Yes, there are plenty of reasons to love winter. And now you have a few more.

W I N T E R

COOKING

Winter cooking is about warmth ... warm foods, of course. But also the warm feelings you generate when the aroma of home-baked bread fills the house. Or a creamy and satisfying soup is served. Or a wonderful pot roast emerges from the oven. Or a special dessert makes its way to table, to the delight of all. So create some winter warmth with these wonderful recipes!

Facing page: Double Chocolate Cake, page 43

Caramelized Onion and Goat Cheese Phyllo Triangles

Served warm, these are some of the best cool-weather appetizers you will ever taste. Look for phyllo dough in the freezer section of the grocery store. Before using, thaw in the refrigerator 6 to 8 hours or overnight. While working with one sheet, cover the others with a barely dampened towel to keep them from drying out. Wrap unused phyllo tightly and refreeze for later use.

2   tablespoons vegetable oil
2   medium onions, thinly sliced
½   teaspoon sugar
½   teaspoon dried thyme
¼   teaspoon salt
⅛   teaspoon freshly ground pepper
1   (3.5- to 4-oz.) pkg. soft goat cheese
4   (14x18-inch) sheets frozen phyllo dough, thawed
5   tablespoons butter, melted

1 In large skillet, heat oil over medium heat until hot. Add onions; sauté onions about 5 minutes, or until slightly softened, stirring occasionally. Reduce heat to low; cover and cook 5 minutes, stirring occasionally. Uncover; add sugar. Cook an additional 10 to 15 minutes or until onions are very soft and golden brown. Add thyme, salt and pepper; mix well. Remove from heat. Let cool. Stir in goat cheese.

2 Heat oven to 400°F. Place 1 sheet of phyllo on cutting board; brush with butter. Cut into 8 (2¼x14-inch) strips. Place 1 teaspoon goat cheese mixture in lower right corner of each strip. Fold corners up and over to enclose filling, forming a triangle. Continue each strip and fold one corner to opposite side to form triangle. Continue to fold, triangle fashion, up length of strip. Brush with melted butter; place on ungreased baking sheet. Repeat with remaining strips, and remaining 3 sheets phyllo.

3 Bake 10 to 12 minutes or until phyllo triangles are browned and crisp. Serve warm or at room temperature.

32 triangles.
Preparation time: 50 minutes.
Ready to serve: 1 hour.
Per triangle: 48 calories, 4 g total fat (2 g saturated fat), 10 mg cholesterol, 50 mg sodium, 0 g fiber.

MOIST BARLEY BREAD

Cooked barley gives a totally different texture than just barley flour. This bread is extremely satisfying with a cup of thick, hot soup on a cold winter evening.

2   (¼-oz.) pkg. active dry yeast
2   tablespoons honey
½   cup warm water (105°F to 115°F)
2   cups lukewarm buttermilk
1   tablespoon light olive or vegetable oil
1   teaspoon salt
½   teaspoon dried rosemary
¼   teaspoon dried thyme
¼   teaspoon baking soda
3   cups unbleached all-purpose flour
2¼ cups whole wheat flour
1   cup cooked pearled barley or wheat berries
    Cornmeal
1   egg beaten with 1 tablespoon milk

1 In large bowl, dissolve yeast and honey in water; let stand 5 minutes. Add buttermilk, oil, salt, rosemary, thyme, baking soda and all-purpose flour; beat at low speed until moistened. With electric mixer, beat 3 minutes at medium speed, scraping bowl occasionally. By hand, stir in whole wheat flour and barley until stiff batter forms.

2 Grease 2 (8x4-inch) loaf pans; sprinkle with cornmeal. Divide batter evenly between pans. Smooth tops of loaves by patting with floured hands. Cover; let rise in warm place 30 minutes or until batter is at top of pans. Heat oven to 400°F. Brush dough with egg mixture; sprinkle with cornmeal. Bake 30 to 35 minutes or until golden brown. Remove from pans; cool on wire rack.

24 servings.
Preparation time: 30 minutes.
Ready to serve: 2 hours.
Per serving: 130 calories, 15 g total fat (0.5 g saturated fat), 10 mg cholesterol, 130 mg sodium, 25 g fiber.

Variation
Kasha Bread
- Substitute cooked kasha (buckwheat groats) for barley. Cook as directed on package.

Baker's Note
- To cook pearled barley or wheat berries, simmer grains in twice the amount of water one hour or until tender. Quick-cooking barley is also available; it takes only 10 minutes to cook.

PERFECT WHITE BREAD DOUGH

Winter is the best season for baking. Here's a recipe for everyday bread that will fill your home with wonderful aromas.

1 (¼-oz.) pkg. active dry yeast
3 cups warm water (105°F to 115°F)
3 tablespoons sugar
⅛ teaspoon ground ginger
6½ to 7 cups unbleached bread flour
⅓ cup nonfat dry milk
2 teaspoons salt
¼ cup butter or lard, softened, plus additional for brushing loaves

1 In small bowl, dissolve yeast in ½ cup of the water. Stir in ½ teaspoon of the sugar and ginger; let stand 10 minutes. In large bowl, combine remaining sugar, 1 cup water, 2 cups of the flour and dry milk, mixing well. Stir in yeast mixture. Cover bowl; let stand 1 hour, until sponge is well risen and bubbly. Stir 1½ cups water, salt and ¼ cup butter into sponge; beat well. Stir in 4 cups flour, mixing until manageable dough forms that clears sides of bowl.

2 Turn dough out onto floured surface. Knead dough 8 to 10 minutes or until smooth and elastic, using as much remaining flour as needed to prevent sticking. Place in greased bowl; turn dough greased side up. Cover; let rise in warm place 1 hour or until doubled in size. Punch dough down. Use as directed in desired recipes or divide in half and freeze in resealable plastic freezer bags.

3 To make loaves, grease 2 (9x5-inch) loaf pans. Punch dough down; turn out onto lightly floured surface. Knead 2 minutes; divide dough in half. Shape into 2 loaves; place in pans. Brush tops of loaves with softened butter. Cover; let rise 45 minutes or until nearly doubled in size. Heat oven to 350°F. Bake 40 minutes or until golden brown. Remove loaves from pans; cool on wire rack.

24 servings.
Preparation time: 3 hours, 35 minutes.
Ready to serve: 4 hours, 15 minutes.
Per serving: 165 calories, 25 g total fat (15 g saturated fat), 5 mg cholesterol, 215 mg sodium, 1 g fiber.

ESCAROLE AND FENNEL SALAD WITH ROASTED GARLIC VINAIGRETTE

Ideal in winter, escarole's bite is complemented by fennel's sweetness. Iceberg lettuce provides a crunchy background, while the roasted garlic vinaigrette pulls everything together.

Vinaigrette
1   head garlic, roasted
⅓   cup extra-virgin olive oil
2   tablespoons red wine vinegar
½   teaspoon Dijon mustard
¼   teaspoon salt
⅛   teaspoon freshly ground pepper

Salad
4   cups bite-size pieces escarole
4   cups bite-size pieces iceberg lettuce
1   medium fennel bulb, fronds removed,
       quartered, cut into ¼-inch slices

1 In blender, combine roasted garlic, oil, vinegar, mustard, salt and pepper. Puree until creamy and well blended.

2 Just before serving, toss escarole, lettuce and fennel bulb with vinaigrette.

6 servings.
Preparation time: 15 minutes.
Ready to serve: 1 hour, 15 minutes.
Per serving: 135 calories, 12 g total fat (15 g saturated fat), 0 mg cholesterol, 130 mg sodium, 2 g fiber.

WINTER SALAD WITH ENDIVE AND CELERY ROOT

Belgian endive and celery root are both popular ingredients in Parisian salads. To prepare ahead, make vinaigrette and assemble lettuce, endive and celery root. To keep the celery root from darkening, toss with enough vinaigrette to coat. Refrigerate vinaigrette, lettuce, endive and celery root. Toss to combine just before serving.

Vinaigrette
- 2 tablespoons Dijon mustard
- 3 tablespoons white wine vinegar
- ⅔ cup vegetable oil
- ¼ teaspoon salt
- ⅛ teaspoon freshly ground pepper

Salad
- 4 cups mixed leaf lettuce
- 1 head Belgian endive, cut into ½-inch slices
- 1 cup diced celery root

1 In small bowl, whisk together mustard and vinegar. Slowly whisk in oil; season with salt and pepper.

2 In large bowl, combine lettuce, endive and celery root. Toss with vinaigrette to coat.

4 servings.
Preparation time: 20 minutes.
Ready to serve: 20 minutes.
Per 4 servings: 360 calories, 37 g total fat (55 g saturated fat), 0 mg cholesterol, 280 mg sodium, 5 g fiber.

HERBED GOAT CHEESE MASHED POTATOES

Goat cheese and fresh herbs dress up a comforting dish of mashed potatoes. This is a nice side dish with chicken or lamb.

2 lb. Yukon Gold potatoes, peeled, cut into 2-inch chunks
8 garlic cloves, peeled
¾ cup reduced-fat milk
2 tablespoons extra-virgin olive oil
4 oz. soft goat cheese, cut into small pieces
¼ cup chopped scallions
3 tablespoons chopped fresh parsley
3 tablespoons chopped fresh chives
½ teaspoon salt
¼ teaspoon freshly ground pepper

1 In large pot, combine potatoes and garlic. Cover with lightly salted water. Bring to a boil over medium-high heat. Reduce heat to medium-low. Simmer, covered, 15 to 20 minutes or until tender. Drain potatoes and return to pot. Shake pot over low heat 1 minute or until potatoes dry slightly. Remove pot from heat.

2 Meanwhile, in 1-cup glass measure, combine milk and oil; microwave on High 1 to 2 minutes or until steaming. (Or heat milk mixture in small saucepan.)

3 Add cheese to potatoes; mash with potato masher. Gradually stir in hot milk mixture to make smooth puree. Gently fold in scallions, parsley, chives, salt and pepper.

6 (¾-cup) servings.
Preparation time: 20 minutes.
Ready to serve: 40 minutes.
Per serving: 230 calories, 9.5 g total fat (4 g saturated fat), 20 mg cholesterol, 285 mg sodium, 3 g fiber.

Chef's Note

- To keep mashed potatoes warm until serving time, set the pan in a larger pan of barely simmering water; place a piece of parchment paper on the surface of the potatoes. You can hold the potatoes like this for up to 1 hour.

SCALLOPED POTATOES

No box here — just wholesome ingredients and full taste. While the potatoes bake on a cold day, enjoy the comforting smells emanating from your oven.

¼   cup melted butter
1   cup sliced white onions (¼ inch)
1   garlic clove, finely minced
2   teaspoons all-purpose flour
1   teaspoon salt
⅛   teaspoon ground white pepper
¼   teaspoon ground nutmeg
6   cups peeled sliced potatoes (¼-inch-thick rounds)
2   cups half-and-half

1 Heat oven to 350°F. Spray 3-quart casserole with nonstick cooking spray.

2 In large skillet, melt butter over medium heat. Add onion slices and garlic; cook until onions are transparent. (Do not brown.)

3 Transfer to shallow bowl. Combine flour, salt, pepper and nutmeg; sprinkle over onion mixture. Toss gently to combine. Place 1 layer potatoes in casserole; top with one-third onion mixture. Build 3 layers and top with half-and-half.

4 Cover and bake 1¼ hours or until potatoes are tender.

4 servings.
Preparation time: 15 minutes.
Ready to serve: 1 hour, 30 minutes.
Per serving: 450 calories, 26 g total fat (16 g saturated fat), 75 mg cholesterol, 720 mg sodium, 45 g fiber.

Chef's Notes

Add one or more of the following if you wish, for an interesting variation:

- 1 cup frankfurters, cut into rounds.
- 1 cup corned beef, cubed to ¼ inch.
- 1 cup fresh mushroom caps cut into ¼-inch slices.
- 1 cup whole kernel corn.
- 1 cup sea legs (crab-flavored fish).
- If you substitute skim milk, the sauce will curdle.

POTATO PANCAKES

These pancakes are culinary poems. You can serve them as a main course at breakfast, as a late supper, or as a wonderful accompaniment to lunch or dinner. Also called *latkes*, these delightful pancakes are Hanukkah traditions.

3 to 4	potatoes, peeled, grated (1½ lb.)
1½	cups peeled grated onions
1	teaspoon lemon juice
1	egg
2	egg yolks
2	tablespoons bread flour
¼	cup Cream of Wheat
1	teaspoon salt
½	teaspoon freshly ground pepper
¼	teaspoon ground nutmeg
1	tablespoon chopped fresh parsley
1½	cups vegetable oil

1 Heat oven to 375°F. In large bowl, combine potatoes, onions and lemon juice. Place in strainer; drain. Set potatoes aside; cover.

2 Add egg and egg yolks to potatoes; mix well. In large bowl, combine flour, Cream of Wheat, salt, pepper, nutmeg and parsley; mix thoroughly. Add to potatoes.

3 In large skillet, heat oil over medium-high heat until hot. For each pancake, pour ½ cup mixture into skillet; lightly press to about ½ inch thick. Cook until lightly brown, turning once.

4 Place pancakes on baking sheet; bake until browned and crisp.

4 servings.
Preparation time: 15 minutes.
Ready to serve: 20 minutes.
Per serving: 340 calories, 13.5 g total fat (2.5 g saturated fat), 160 mg cholesterol, 650 mg sodium, 4.5 g fiber.

Chef's Notes

- If you prefer, you can fry the pancakes until they are browned and crisp, rather than baking them.
- If you are making potato pancakes in advance, it is best to finish them in the oven.

WILD RICE AND MUSHROOM SOUP

Wild rice adds a wonderful, nutty flavor to this soup. Pancetta is a cured, unsmoked Italian bacon. If unavailable, substitute regular bacon, simmering it in water for 10 minutes to remove the smoky flavor. Drain and thoroughly pat dry before using. This soup is hearty enough to be the main course of any winter dinner. Pair it up with a good loaf of bread (like *Perfect White Bread*, page 12).

1 (1-oz.) pkg. dried wild mushrooms
1 cup very hot water (115°F to 120°F)
1 tablespoon vegetable oil
1 cup diced pancetta
¼ cup chopped shallots or green onions
1 (8-oz.) pkg. mushrooms, sliced
⅓ cup all-purpose flour
2 cups milk
1 (14.5-oz.) can chicken broth (or an additional 2 cups milk plus ¾ teaspoon salt)
2 cups cooked wild rice

1 Soak dried mushrooms in very hot water in medium bowl 30 minutes. Remove mushrooms; chop. Strain soaking liquid through coffee filter to remove grit; set aside.

2 Heat oil in Dutch oven over medium-high heat until hot. Add pancetta; sauté 1 minute. Add shallots; sauté 3 to 5 minutes or until tender and pancetta is browned. Add mushrooms; sauté 5 to 8 minutes or until tender. Add chopped wild mushrooms and reserved soaking liquid. Cook 5 minutes or until all liquid is absorbed. Stir in flour; whisk in milk and broth. Bring to a boil; continue cooking, stirring, for several minutes to thicken. Stir in rice; reduce heat to low. Simmer 5 minutes.

4 servings.
Preparation time: 30 minutes.
Ready to serve: 1 hour, 20 minutes.
Per main course serving: 295 calories, 11 g total fat (35 g saturated fat), 15 mg cholesterol, 905 mg sodium, 3 g fiber.

Grandma's Chicken Noodle Soup

Comforting homemade soup may be just what the doctor ordered when you need it most.

This is a soul-warming soup that you'll want to make over and over again.

2 tablespoons butter, softened
1 small onion, finely chopped
1 carrot, diced
1 rib celery, finely chopped
¼ cup all-purpose flour
2 quarts chicken broth
1 (4-oz.) pkg. egg noodles
¼ cup half-and-half
½ teaspoon ground white pepper
2 cups shredded cooked chicken
   Chopped fresh parsley

1 In large pot, heat butter over medium-high heat until melted; add onions. Cook 3 minutes or until tender. Stir in carrot and celery; cook an additional 5 minutes. Stir in flour; mix until well blended. Cook, stirring constantly, an additional 1 minute.

2 Add broth, stirring vigorously. Adjust heat to high and bring broth to a boil. Add noodles and cook 10 minutes or until noodles are al dente.

3 Stir in half-and-half, pepper and chicken; heat thoroughly. Garnish with parsley.

6 cups.
Preparation time: 18 minutes.
Ready to serve: 30 minutes.
Per cup: 265 calories, 10 g total fat (45 g saturated fat), 675 mg cholesterol, 155 mg sodium, 2 g fiber.

CREAMY THREE-POTATO SOUP

Soups can be creamy without a lot of added fat. The pureed potatoes give this soup a rich, velvety texture accented by the subtle flavor of leeks. To clean leeks, trim off root ends and cut the stalks in half lengthwise. Separate sections under running water to remove grit. This soup makes a heart-warming beginning to any winter meal.

2	tablespoons vegetable oil
2	medium leeks, chopped, white and light green portions only
1	medium onion, sliced
6	cups reduced-sodium chicken broth
½	lb. russet potatoes, peeled, sliced
½	lb. Yukon Gold potatoes, peeled, sliced
1	lb. sweet potatoes or yams, peeled, sliced
½	cup milk
¼	teaspoon ground white pepper

1 Heat oil in Dutch oven over medium heat until hot. Sauté leeks and onion 3 to 4 minutes. Add broth and potatoes; bring to a boil. Reduce heat to low; simmer, partially covered, about 30 to 40 minutes, or until tender. Remove from heat; cool slightly. Puree in blender or food processor; return to Dutch oven. Stir in milk and pepper. Heat gently over low heat just until hot.

6 servings.
Preparation time: 25 minutes.
Ready to serve: 1 hour.

Per main course serving: 225 calories, 65 g total fat (15 g saturated fat), 0 mg cholesterol, 505 mg sodium, 4 g fiber.

LENTIL-ORZO STEW

Serve this wonderful stew in wide pasta bowls accompanied with toasted country bread and some good olive oil for dipping. Comfort food at its very best!

1	tablespoon olive oil
2	cups onions, chopped
1	cup finely chopped carrots
6	garlic cloves, minced
1¼	cups brown lentils, rinsed
1	tablespoon chopped fresh thyme or 1 teaspoon dried
6	cups vegetable or reduced-sodium chicken broth
½	cup water
1	bay leaf
1¼	cups orzo
1	(14.5-oz.) can diced tomatoes, undrained
¾	teaspoon salt
¼	teaspoon freshly ground pepper
2 to 3	tablespoons fresh lemon juice
2	teaspoons butter
⅓	cup chopped fresh Italian parsley

1 In large pot or Dutch oven, heat oil over medium heat until hot. Add onions and carrots; cook 4 to 6 minutes or until tender, stirring frequently. Add garlic; cook and stir 1 minute. Stir in lentils and thyme. Add broth, water and bay leaf. Bring to a boil. Reduce heat to low; simmer, covered, 20 minutes.

2 Add orzo; simmer, covered, 15 minutes or until lentils and orzo are almost tender, stirring occasionally.

3 Add tomatoes; simmer, covered, 10 to 15 minutes or until lentils and orzo are tender, stirring occasionally. (Add about ½ cup water if stew begins to stick.) Remove and discard bay leaf.

4 Stir in salt and pepper. (Stew can be made ahead. Cover and refrigerate up to 2 days. Reheat over medium-low heat, adding enough water to achieve stew-like consistency.) Stir in lemon juice, butter and parsley.

8 (1⅓-cups) servings.
Preparation time: 20 minutes.
Ready to serve: 1 hour, 15 minutes.
Per serving: 270 calories, 45 g total fat (15 g saturated fat), 5 mg cholesterol, 670 mg sodium, 10 g fiber.

PROVENCAL BEEF STEW WITH OLIVES

Here is a robust, make-ahead stew you can proudly serve to company. Accompany with egg noodles. And don't forget to pick up some good crusty bread to soak up the delicious sauce.

1   (3½-lb.) beef chuck roast, trimmed, cut into 1¾-inch pieces
1   (750-ml) bottle dry red wine
1   teaspoon black peppercorns, crushed
8   fresh thyme sprigs or 1 teaspoon dried
8   fresh Italian parsley stems (reserve leaves for garnish)
2   (2x½-inch) strips orange peel
1   bay leaf
2   tablespoons olive oil, divided
2   cups chopped onions
1   cup chopped carrots
4   garlic cloves, minced
1   (28-oz.) can plum tomatoes, drained
¼   teaspoon freshly ground pepper
⅔   cup niçoise olives, pitted
¼   teaspoon salt, if desired
½   cup chopped fresh Italian parsley

1   In large resealable plastic bag, combine beef, wine and peppercorns; seal bag. Refrigerate at least 2 hours or overnight.

2   Heat oven to 300°F. With butcher's twine, tie thyme, parsley, orange peel and bay leaf together in piece of cheesecloth to make a bouquet garni. Set aside.

3   Drain beef, reserving marinade. Dry beef with paper towels. Heat oil in nonreactive Dutch oven over medium-high heat until hot. Brown beef in batches 2 to 4 minutes or until well browned on all sides. Remove from Dutch oven; set aside.

4   Add onions and carrots to Dutch oven; cook 4 to 6 minutes or until tender and lightly browned, stirring frequently. Add garlic; cook and stir about 30 seconds. Add reserved marinade. Bring to a boil, stirring to scrape up any browned bits. Add beef, tomatoes, pepper and bouquet garni. Bring to a boil over medium-high heat.

5   Bake, covered, 2½ hours or until beef is almost tender.

6   Add olives to stew; bake an additional 20 to 30 minutes or until beef is very tender.

7   With slotted spoon, transfer beef and olives to serving dish; keep warm. Discard bouquet garni. Skim fat from top of sauce with paper towels. If desired, boil sauce over high heat 5 to 10 minutes to intensify flavor and thicken slightly. Add salt. Pour sauce over beef and olives. (Stew can be made up to 2 days ahead. Cover and refrigerate. Reheat gently on stovetop before serving.) Garnish with parsley.

6 (1¼-cups) servings.
Preparation time: 45 minutes.
Ready to serve: 6 hours.
Per serving: 550 calories, 30.5 g total fat (10.5 g saturated fat), 140 mg cholesterol, 485 mg sodium, 35 g fiber.

Chef's Notes

- A bouquet garni is an essential flavoring element in long-simmered meat stews. In addition to the standard parsley, thyme and bay leaf, this bouquet includes orange peel, which gives this stew a distinctive Provençal flavor.

- Tangy and delicate, niçoise olives are small, dark brownish purple brine-cured olives from France. Look for them in specialty stores.

CHORIZO CHILI

What could be better than a bountiful chili on a winter day? Chorizo is a type of sausage found in Mexican and southwestern cooking. Feel free to substitute a spicy Italian sausage if unavailable. Use canned tomatoes for convenience when fresh aren't available.

1	tablespoon vegetable oil
½	lb. chorizo or other spicy sausage, sliced
1	large onion, chopped (1 cup)
1	green pepper, chopped
1	tablespoon minced garlic
1	(28-oz.) can diced tomatoes, undrained, or 2 pounds chopped fresh tomatoes
1	(15-oz.) can kidney beans, rinsed, drained
1	(14.5-oz) can beef broth
2	tablespoons chili powder
1	teaspoon ground cumin
½	teaspoon dried oregano
⅛	teaspoon cayenne pepper
1	cup corn

1 Heat nonreactive Dutch oven or large pot over medium-high heat. Add oil; heat until hot. Add chorizo; sauté 2 to 3 minutes or until chorizo begins to brown. Add onion, green pepper and garlic; sauté 3 to 4 minutes or until vegetables begin to soften. Add tomatoes, beans, broth, chili powder, cumin, oregano and cayenne pepper; mix well. Bring to a boil; reduce heat to low. Simmer, partially covered, 20 minutes. Add corn; cook an additional 10 minutes.

4 servings.
Preparation time: 15 minutes.
Ready to serve: 40 minutes.
Per serving: 475 calories, 27 g total fat (9 g saturated fat), 50 mg cholesterol, 1755 mg sodium, 9 g fiber.

THE FISHERMAN'S WIFE'S POT PIE

You may add different kinds of fish pieces, shrimp or scallops to this pie. It makes for a superb one-dish meal.

¼ cup butter
½ cup diced red onions (¼ inch thick)
1 cup sliced carrots (¼-inch-thick half moons)
1 cup diced potatoes (½ inch thick)
½ cup sherry wine
1 cup seeded diced tomatoes (½ inch thick)
1 cup sliced fresh green beans (1 inch long)
½ cup diced mushrooms (½ inch thick)
2 cup diced boneless, skinless fish fillets (1 inch thick)
3 egg yolks
4 cups heavy cream
¼ cup all-purpose flour
¼ teaspoon ground nutmeg
½ teaspoon salt
¼ teaspoon ground white pepper
1 teaspoon fresh thyme or ½ teaspoon dried
2 teaspoons fresh tarragon or 1 teaspoon dried
1 prepared (9-inch) pie crust

1 Heat oven to 350°F.

2 In large skillet, heat butter to a fast bubble over medium-high heat. Add onions and carrots; sauté 3 minutes, stirring gently to keep from sticking. Stir in potatoes and sherry. Reduce heat to low; simmer 10 minutes. Remove from heat.

3 Stir in tomatoes, green beans and mushrooms. Place mixture in Dutch oven or 3-quart casserole. Top with fish pieces.

4 In medium bowl, combine egg yolks, cream, flour, nutmeg; salt, pepper, thyme, tarragon, and mix well until smooth. Pour over fish. Top with prepared pie crust; press to seal crust edges to edges of Dutch oven. Cut small hole in center for steam to escape. Brush crust evenly with cream to enhance browning. Bake 1 hour.

4 servings.
Preparation time: 45 minutes.
Ready to serve: 1 hour, 45 minutes.
Per serving: 40 calories, 105 g total fat (60 g saturated fat), 500 mg cholesterol, 700 mg sodium, 4 g fiber.

Chef's Note
• Use heavy cream or the sauce will curdle.

MACARONI AND CHEESE WITH TOMATOES AND FONTINA

Who can resist good macaroni and cheese? It's not just for kids, you know. Here, tomatoes contribute a lively, acidic element. Vegetarians can omit the pancetta, or replace it with minced and sautéed portobello mushrooms.

1 tablespoon kosher (coarse) salt plus more to taste
1 lb. canneroni, trennete or other medium tube pasta
6 oz. pancetta, minced
1 (12-oz.) can evaporated milk
½ cup whipping cream
1 (14-oz.) can diced tomatoes
1 tablespoon hot pepper sauce
   Freshly ground pepper to taste
5 cups shredded or grated Monterey Jack cheese (20 oz.)
3 cups shredded or grated Italian fontina cheese (12 oz.)
2 cups fresh bread crumbs, toasted

1 Fill large pot two-thirds full of water; add 1 tablespoon salt. Bring to a boil over high heat. Cook canneroni according to package directions; drain. Do not rinse.

2 Meanwhile, in medium skillet over medium heat, sauté pancetta until translucent, about 5 minutes. Remove from heat; set aside.

3 Heat oven to 350°F. In large bowl, combine evaporated milk, cream, tomatoes and hot pepper sauce. Season with pepper. Fold in cheeses. Add pasta and pancetta to cheese mixture; stir together gently but thoroughly.

4 Pour pasta mixture into 3½-quart casserole. Season bread crumbs with salt and pepper; spread over pasta. Cover tightly with aluminum foil; bake 20 minutes. Remove foil; bake an additional 10 minutes or until bread crumbs are lightly toasted. Remove from oven; let stand 5 minutes before serving.

8 servings.
Preparation time: 15 minutes.
Ready to serve: 45 minutes.
Per serving: 1275 calories, 85 g total fat (45 g saturated fat), 210 mg cholesterol, 1660 mg sodium, 4 g fiber.

HONEY-GLAZED BAKED HAM

This is the best way to make a ham for company. Let it cook all afternoon while you and your guests play cards, watch a football game or just visit the day away.

Honey Glaze

1	cup dill pickle juice
1	cup packed brown sugar
1	tablespoon yellow mustard
½	teaspoon ground cloves
¼	teaspoon ground cinnamon
½	cup honey
1	cup pineapple juice
½	cup chopped onions
¼	teaspoon cayenne pepper
¼	cup cornstarch

Ham

1	(45-lb.) shank half ham, bone-in

1 In blender, combine pickle juice, brown sugar, mustard, cloves, cinnamon, honey, pineapple juice, onions, cayenne pepper and cornstarch; process until smooth. Pour mixture into large pot; bring to a slow boil. Simmer 5 minutes on low heat, stirring constantly.

2 Heat oven to 300°F. Remove excess fat and skin from ham. Place ham on baking rack in roasting pan. Score ham on all sides. For appearance, press whole clove into each scored square.

3 Bake uncovered 2 hours. With pastry brush, baste top of ham with light coating of honey glaze. Repeat every 10 to 15 minutes up to 1 hour or until internal temperature reaches 175°F.

4 Transfer ham to serving platter. Brush with last thick layer of glaze. Reheat remaining glaze to boiling; serve as sauce. Slice ham and serve with hot glaze in sauce boat.

8 servings.
Preparation time: 15 minutes.
Ready to serve: 4 hours, 15 minutes.
Per serving: 540 calories, 17 g total fat (6 g saturated fat), 115 mg cholesterol, 3060 mg sodium, 0.5 g fiber.

Chef's Notes

- The glaze will not permeate the meat, but it does give the meat a great appearance and tasty outer crust. This glaze may also be used with chicken or pork chops.

- Remove whole cloves before serving.

- A boneless turkey breast is excellent roasted this way.

GARLIC-ROASTED CHICKEN BITES WITH TEQUILA DIP

Fresh boneless chicken thighs taste the very best here, but the frozen variety will do. This looks like a lot of garlic, but it becomes quite mild during cooking. You'll smell it, though!

Chicken
2 teaspoons freshly ground pepper
1 teaspoon kosher (coarse) salt
½ teaspoon ground coriander
6 garlic cloves, minced
1 lb. boneless skinless chicken thighs, cut into 1 ½-inch pieces
3 tablespoons minced fresh cilantro

Tequila Dip
2 garlic cloves
⅓ cup ketchup
1 tablespoon packed brown sugar
1 tablespoon white or cider vinegar
1 tablespoon Tequila or fresh lime juice
½ cup raisins

1 Heat oven to 500°F.

2 In medium bowl, combine pepper, salt, coriander and garlic; mix well. Toss chicken pieces in mixture until well coated. Spray 15x10x1-inch pan with nonstick cooking spray. Arrange chicken in single layer in pan.

3 Bake 18 to 20 minutes or until chicken is no longer pink in center.

4 Meanwhile, prepare Tequila Dip: In food processor, combine garlic, ketchup, brown sugar, vinegar, Tequila and raisins until sauce is blended and raisins are coarsely chopped.

5 Sprinkle chicken with cilantro. Insert toothpick in each chicken bite; serve with Tequila Dip.

16 chicken bites.
Preparation time: 30 minutes.
Ready to serve: 50 minutes.
Per serving: 70 calories, 2 g total fat (1 g saturated fat), 19 mg cholesterol, 175 mg sodium, 1 g fiber.

POT ROAST

There's nothing like a pot roast to warm your soul on a frigid, windy day. Make the largest roast you can so that you generate plenty of leftovers for such delights as hot pot roast sandwiches.

1	(3- to 3½-lb.) boneless game roast
¼	cup vegetable oil
2	cups chopped onions (1 inch)
1½	cups chopped carrots (1 inch)
1½	cups chopped rutabaga (1 inch)
3	tablespoons all-purpose flour
⅔	cup dark raisins
2	teaspoons dried thyme
3	cups beef broth
½	cup dark rum
1	cup chili sauce
1	tablespoon beef base
⅓	cup molasses
1	teaspoon freshly ground pepper
1	cup red wine
1	tablespoon Worcestershire sauce
2	teaspoons cornstarch

1 Heat oven to 350°F.

2 Remove excess fat and silver skin from roast. In Dutch oven, heat oil over medium heat until hot. Add roast; brown on all sides, about 10 minutes. Remove roast and set aside.

3 Add onions, carrots and rutabaga; cook until light brown, about 5 minutes. Add flour; cook 3 minutes, stirring constantly.

4 Return roast to Dutch oven. Stir in raisins, thyme, beef broth, rum, chili sauce, beef base, molasses and pepper.

5 Bake 2 hours. In small bowl, combine red wine, Worcestershire sauce and cornstarch to make smooth paste. Add to pot; stir to combine. Bake an additional 30 minutes. Remove meat; slice into thick pieces. Serve with vegetable sauce, if desired.

6 servings.
Preparation time: 30 minutes.
Ready to serve: 3 hours, 30 minutes.
Per serving: 595 calories, 16 g total fat (4 g saturated fat), 190 mg cholesterol, 660 mg sodium, 45 g fiber.

Chef's Note
- It is important to brown the roast well to caramelize the meat sugars. This will add extra flavor.

HOT ROASTED CHICKEN AND POTATOES

If your family loves take-out fried chicken, they will love this even more! Cook potatoes at the same time in the hot oven, and you've got a meal that's delicious, as well as very healthy and low in fat. What's more, the recipe is quick and easy to make, which means it's perfect for a busy evening.

1½	lb. boneless skinless chicken thighs
5	tablespoons olive oil
⅓	cup brown rice flour
1½	teaspoons salt
¼	teaspoon freshly ground pepper
¼	teaspoon dried rosemary
2	lb. potatoes, cut into spears
2	teaspoons kosher (coarse) salt

1 Heat oven to 550°F. Rinse chicken and pat dry. Brush with 2 tablespoons of the oil.

2 In medium bowl, combine flour, salt, pepper and rosemary; mix well. Toss chicken in mixture until coated.

3 In another medium bowl, toss potatoes with remaining 3 tablespoons oil; sprinkle with salt.

4 Cover large, shallow, heavy roasting pan with aluminum foil. Arrange chicken pieces and potato wedges on aluminum foil.

5 Bake chicken and potatoes 20 minutes or until chicken is no longer pink in center.

4 servings.
Preparation time: 10 minutes.
Ready to serve: 20 minutes.
Per serving: 535 calories, 245 g total fat (45 g saturated fat), 75 mg cholesterol, 1295 mg sodium, 45 g fiber.

TURKEY TERRINE WITH PINE NUTS

Not just for appetizers, this terrine makes a great first course, too! Slice and serve on a leaf of lettuce along with a tasty mustard. Or place thin slices on dark pumpernickel bread, spread with mustard and cut into small squares or triangles to serve as an appetizer or canapé.

2	tablespoons butter, softened
1	onion, finely chopped
2	garlic cloves, minced
¼	lb. fresh mushrooms, chopped
¼	cup brandy
3	eggs
1	cup fresh whole-grain bread crumbs
½	teaspoon ground allspice
½	teaspoon dried thyme
½	teaspoon salt
1¼	lb. lean ground turkey
½	lb. cooked turkey ham, cut into ½-inch pieces
⅔	cup pine nuts

1 Heat oven to 325°F. Spray 6-cup loaf pan with nonstick cooking spray. Cut strip of parchment paper the same length as the pan; place in pan, allowing excess to hang over edge.

2 In large skillet, melt butter over medium-high heat. Add onion and garlic; sauté 2 minutes or until onion is tender. Add mushrooms; continue cooking about 1 minute, stirring occasionally until liquid evaporates.

3 Add brandy; simmer 1 minute.

4 In large bowl, combine eggs, bread crumbs, allspice, thyme, salt and mushroom mixture; mix well. Add turkey, ham and ⅓ cup of the pine nuts; mix until well blended.

5 Press mixture into prepared pan. Top with remaining ⅓ cup pine nuts. Press overlapping parchment paper over top of meat mixture; cover tightly with aluminum foil or terrine lid.

6 Place pan in larger pan; add water to larger pan measuring about halfway up sides of small pan. Bake 2½ hours or until internal temperature reaches 180°F.

7 Cool on wire rack. Cover meatloaf and chill 4 hours.

12 servings.
Preparation time: 2 hours, 30 minutes.
Ready to serve: 4 hours.
Per serving: 210 calories, 13 g total fat (4 g saturated fat), 100 mg cholesterol, 370 mg sodium, 15 g fiber.

Sweet-and-Sour Turkey Tenderloin

To add to the Asian theme of this dish, add a vegetable stir-fry to the menu. What a fun
and different way to cook holiday turkey!

1   lb. turkey tenderloin
⅔   cup cornstarch
½   teaspoon salt
1   egg, beaten
2   tablespoons vegetable oil
1   medium onion, cut into 8 wedges
1   green bell pepper, cut into 1-inch pieces
1   medium tomato, chopped
1   (8-oz.) can pineapple chunks, drained
½   cup prepared sweet and sour sauce
3   cups rice, steamed

1 Rinse turkey and pat dry. Cut turkey into 1½-inch cubes.

2 In resealable plastic bag, combine cornstarch and salt; shake to mix.

3 In large bowl, roll turkey in egg. Add turkey to cornstarch mixture in bag; shake until well coated. Set aside.

4 In large skillet, heat 1 tablespoon of the oil over medium-high heat until hot. Add onion and bell pepper; sauté 5 to 6 minutes or until onion is tender and transparent. Remove from pan; set aside.

5 Add remaining 1 tablespoon oil and turkey to skillet; brown and drain, if necessary. Add onion, bell pepper, tomato, pineapple and sweet and sour sauce. Cook until turkey is no longer pink in center. Serve over rice.

4 servings.
Preparation time: 10 minutes.
Ready to serve: 15 minutes.
Per serving: 631 calories, 21.7 g total fat (3.9 g saturated fat), 93.8 mg cholesterol, 922 mg sodium, 2.3 g fiber.

WHITE SUGAR COOKIES

Don't rely on a tube of dough from the supermarket when you want to bake up a batch of sugar cookies. This recipe makes the job easier — and the cookies better!

½   cup shortening
½   cup butter, softened
1   cup sugar
2   eggs
1   teaspoon vanilla
3   cups all-purpose flour
2   teaspoons cream of tartar
1   teaspoon baking soda
¼   teaspoon salt
3   tablespoons heavy cream, whipped

1 Heat oven to 375°F. Spray several baking sheets with nonstick cooking spray.

2 In large bowl, beat shortening, butter and sugar at medium speed 2 minutes. Add eggs and vanilla; beat at medium speed until thoroughly combined. In large bowl, sift flour, cream of tartar, baking soda and salt; blend into shortening mixture with cream. Refrigerate at least 2 hours.

3 Roll dough ⅛ inch thick onto flour-dusted bread board. Cut with 3-inch cookie cutter; arrange dough about 1 inch apart on baking sheets.

4 Bake 6 to 8 minutes or until golden. Store cookies in airtight container.

4 dozen cookies.
Preparation time: 20 minutes.
Ready to serve: 1 hour.
Per serving: 90 calories, 45 g total fat (2 g saturated fat), 15 mg cholesterol, 55 mg sodium, 0 g fiber.

Chef's Note
- Use this recipe to make your Christmas and Holiday cookies. Snowmen, angels, stars, santas, Christmas trees and all the traditional shapes are great!

CANDIED APPLES

These *Candied Apples* are great as a side dish with duck, goose or pork.

1   cup packed brown sugar
2   tablespoons butter
6   Granny Smith apples
     Dash salt

1 In large skillet, combine brown sugar and butter; heat until sugar is dissolved. Add apples and salt. Cook uncovered over very low heat about 1 hour, turning frequently until softened; serve.

8 servings.
Preparation time: 15 minutes.
Ready to serve: 1 hour 15 minutes.
Per serving: 190 calories, 3 g total fat (2 g saturated fat), 8 mg cholesterol, 65 mg sodium, 3 g fiber.

DOUBLE CHOCOLATE CAKE

Those of us who love chocolate know — double the chocolate and the cake DOES get doubly better! This is the perfect, down-home dessert after a warm winter meal ... or serve with coffee later. Of course, the kids will love it too.

Cake

¾	cup butter
½	teaspoon salt
2	teaspoons vanilla
2¼	cups sugar
3	eggs
3	(1-oz.) squares unsweetened chocolate
2½	cups cake flour
¾	teaspoon baking powder
1½	teaspoons baking soda
1¼	cups cold water
¼	cup crème de cocoa

Frosting

1½	cups packed brown sugar
1	tablespoon crème de cocoa
¼	cup butter
1	cup semisweet chocolate chips (6 oz.)
6	tablespoons heavy cream, whipped

1 Heat oven to 350°F. Spray 13x9-inch pan with nonstick cooking spray; lightly flour.

2 In large bowl, beat together butter, salt, vanilla and sugar at medium speed 3 minutes. Add eggs, one at a time, beating 20 seconds after each addition.

3 Melt chocolate in double boiler or microwave. Add slowly to batter; beat 30 seconds.

4 In another large bowl, sift together flour, baking powder and baking soda; add alternately with cold water and crème de cocoa. Beat 1 minute; pour batter into pan.

5 Bake 40 to 45 minutes or until toothpick inserted near center comes out clean. Let cool on wire rack before frosting.

6 To prepare Frosting: boil brown sugar, crème de cocoa and butter in medium pot 1 minute. Add chocolate chips and cream; stir until melted and smooth. Cool; spread over cake.

12 servings.
Preparation time: 20 minutes.
Ready to serve: 40 minutes.
Per slice: 660 calories, 28 g total fat (17 g saturated fat), 105 mg cholesterol, 430 mg sodium, 25 g fiber.

BREAD PUDDING

Here's a delicious bread pudding — warm, sweet and satisfying at any time of year, but especially appealing when winter's winds blow outside and you're all cozied up inside.

Pudding

6	eggs
3	egg yolks
¾	cup packed brown sugar
1	quart half-and-half
2	teaspoons vanilla
½	cup melted butter
½	teaspoon ground nutmeg
¼	teaspoon ground cinnamon
6	cups cubed sweet rolls (1½ inches)
½	cup raisins

Sauce

1	lb. packed brown sugar
¾	cup water
⅔	cup corn syrup
½	cup butter
1	tablespoon vanilla
2	cups heavy cream, whipped
½	cup orange-flavored liqueur

Chef's Note

- For bread cubes: beforehand save and freeze leftover doughnuts, sweet rolls, caramel rolls and Danish rolls. The more caramel and filling they have, the better the flavor.
- The liqueur sauce keeps well if refrigerated. Heat in a small pot when needed. It is important to have and use a candy thermometer. It takes a long time for the sauce to reach 320°F!
- The sauce is also wonderful over ice cream or freshly-cut apple wedges.

1 Heat oven to 375°F.

2 In large bowl, beat eggs and yolks at medium speed until frothy.

3 In another large bowl, cream brown sugar, half-and-half, vanilla, butter, nutmeg and cinnamon; blend well with wire whisk. Add cubed sweet rolls and raisins; let stand 15 minutes. Gently mix, being careful not to break up bread cubes. Pour into 8-inch round cake pan. Place 8-inch round cake pan into 9-inch round cake pan. Place pans in oven, filling 9-inch pan as full as possible with hot water.

4 Using another 8-inch round cake pan, trace bottom of pan along parchment paper; butter 8-inch round parchment. Cover pudding with buttered parchment; bake 1½ hours or until knife inserted near center comes out clean. Serve hot with sauce.

5 To prepare Sauce: Place brown sugar, water and corn syrup in medium saucepan; bring to a fast boil until candy thermometer reaches 320°F, about 10 minutes. Reduce heat to low; add butter, vanilla and orange-flavored liqueur, stirring well with wooden spoon. Remove from heat. Add cream, stirring until smooth with wooden spoon. Serve hot over pudding.

16 servings.
Preparation time: 25 minutes.
Ready to serve: 1 hour, 30 minutes.
Per serving: 400 calories, 245 g total fat (135 g saturated fat), 180 mg cholesterol, 160 mg sodium, .5 g fiber.

HOT BUTTERED CIDER

This hot beverage is perfect for chilly winter evenings. For children, or guests who avoid alcohol, omit the rum and butter.

2   quarts apple cider
8   sticks cinnamon
8   whole cloves
8   allspice berries
3   (quarter-sized) slices peeled fresh ginger
4   slices lemon, halved
¼   cup sugar
¾   cup dark rum
8   teaspoons butter

1 In Dutch oven or large pot, heat cider, cinnamon, cloves, allspice berries, ginger, lemon and sugar over medium heat about 10 minutes or until boiling. Reduce heat to low; simmer 10 minutes to develop flavors. Strain, reserving lemon slices and cinnamon sticks. Cover and refrigerate, if desired; reheat before serving.

2 Measure 3 tablespoons rum into each of 8 (12-ounce) mugs. Ladle 1 cup hot cider into each mug, including cinnamon stick and lemon slice half if desired. Float 1 teaspoon pat of butter on surface of each mug.

8 servings
Preparation time: 20 minutes.
Ready to serve: 25 minutes.
Per triangle: 225 calories, 4 g total fat (2.5 g saturated fat), 10 mg cholesterol, 35 mg sodium, 0.5 g fiber.

WINTER

CRAFTS

Winter was made for crafting. Or maybe crafting was made for winter. Either way, cold days make it fun to be indoors, getting creative and making wonderful items for your home, your friends, your family and yourself. Most of these craft ideas are geared to either the season or its holidays. But that's only fitting. Because winter itself gives a person many reasons to celebrate!

Facing page: Polar Fleece Mittens, page 64

Tag Art Holiday Greeting

Gather luggage tags, items from home and nature, and pretty ribbon, then get creative and make an attractive holiday greeting for shelf or mantel. Create any message you want — long or short, or geared to Christmas, Hanukkah, New Years — whatever holiday is important to you.

Hang this unique holiday greeting on your door, wall or over a picture frame. It is made using thin cardboard luggage tags, available in office supply stores. Then put a letter on each to spell out a holiday greeting such as PEACE or NOEL, or a winter or year-round greeting.

Each letter is formed with a different element such as buttons, seeds, twigs, leaves, flower petals, crushed rose petals, small ribbon roses or seed beads, or use calligraphy if you wish.

Use the extra luggage tags for gift labels using the above elements to decorate them, such as making a ribbon rose heart on a valentine gift tag. Another good use for extra labels is to label storage boxes.

Since a lot of the elements can be found in nature or at home, the cost for this project is minimal. Elements can be adhered either by using a glue gun, white glue or a glue stick. Choose the best method according to the weight and flexibility of the element. Making your own letters is easy, because a simple stick letter will work, since the letter tracing should not show. The thickness of the letters depends on the element being used; however, strive for about ½ inch thick.

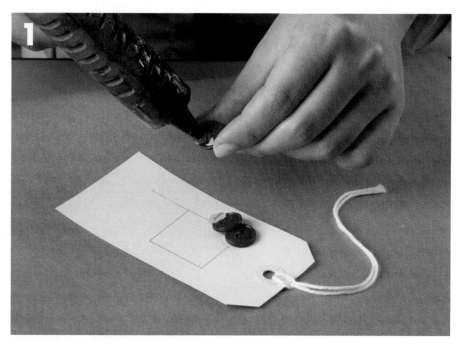

1 Lightly trace letters centered on tag. For some of the elements being applied it is just as easy to make stick letters down the center of where the letter is to be. Do not put any pencil lines where they will not be covered, as they are hard to remove later. Determine which letters you want covered with which elements. Study the shape of the letter and the elements to see which most naturally follow the lines. Also determine the best way to glue each element. Larger, less pliable elements like twigs, stiff leaves and buttons can be adhered best with the glue gun, as in the E and P. Arrange buttons as desired to make sure there are enough. Buttons can be identical or mix and match. However, keep them in the same color range for readability. For the buttons, put glue from glue gun on button and a bit on the tag. For the twigs and leaves, it is easiest to run a line of glue on the tag and then adhere the twig or leaf. Do not use a lot of glue to avoid it showing.

2 For more delicate and small items, such as petals or seeds, use white glue or a glue stick. The white glue from a bottle is best applied by using a brush. For rose petals adequate glue is needed on the tag. Brush it on the width of the brush and brush a bit on the wrong side of petal, close to the edges. When adhering the rose petal hold it in place a moment. Continue forming the letter. For birdseed, apply white glue to the tag. Place tag in a plastic lid and pour seeds over tag. Lightly press seeds. Remove tag. Seeds can be pushed around a bit to fill in or remove from an area. Also dabs of glue can be put in areas and more seeds added.

3 Let glue dry well for all letters. Remove string from tag holes and replace with narrow red ribbon, each one about 16 inches long, folded in half and looped into tag hole. Use a relatively straight larger twig to hang the letters. Use a monofilament line, ribbon or hooks to hang twig.

WOODEN ADVENT TREE

Don't get rid of your traditional wall or window advent calendar. Just add to the idea with this unique and fun advent tree.

Traditional Advent calendars hang on the wall and are made of cardboard or fabric. For a new twist, make a small wooden tree as an Advent calendar. It is easy to make using dowels and is decorated with miniature ornaments. The paint is partially sanded off to give a worn or antique effect.

Keep ornaments under the tree in a small decorative box and put one ornament on the tree each day in December, until the 25th, when the final ornament, the star at the top, is put in place. The height of the tree is about 14 inches and the widest part of the tree is 7½ inches.

To expand the tree's size, place the dowels farther apart and make them longer. A flatter version can be made for a mantel or narrower space, by dividing the length of the main dowel (trunk) into eight and only using six of them, eliminating the front and back mark.

1 Cut ⅝-inch dowel to 14 or 15 inches. Cut ¼-inch dowels in the following lengths: 7½, 7, 6½, 6, 5½, 5, 4½, 4, 3½, 3, 2½ and 2 inches. At top end of ⅝-inch dowel, divide it into 6 equal pie shapes. Extend one line down to other end. Make the same size pie shapes on the other end. Then connect the remaining five lines down the length of the dowel.

Starting at the top, measure ¾ inch down one of the lines and mark. Measure 1 inch down from that line and over to the next line and mark. Continue doing this until there are 12 marks spiraling down the dowel. Drill ¼-inch holes at the marks. Line up lines on end of dowel vertical with drill bit. Hold dowel tight while drilling. To prevent splintering, drill almost all the way through and then turn and drill from the other side. Sand cut ends of all pieces and drilled areas.

Materials & Tools

- ⅝-inch dowel — 15 inches long
- ¼-inch dowel — 5 feet long
- Small scrap of 1 by 6 piece of wood (to make a 4½-inch square and a 5½-inch square)
- Spray paint — Christmas green, gold (the gold paint can be acrylic craft paint)
- Spray matte acrylic sealer
- 24 miniature ornaments
- Wood star — 1 inch by ½ inch
- Four 1¼-inch-long nails or flathead screws
- Drill press
- Radial arm saw
- Wood (optional)

Craft Tip

- Being able to use a drill press ensures a more accurate result, as does having an extra person to help hold the dowels as they are being drilled.

2 Create wood base, by cutting two squares from scrap of 1 by 6, measuring 4½ inches square and 5½ inches square. Sand edges to smooth them. Center smaller square over larger square; clamp together. Turn pieces over and nail together or drill four holes and screw together. On top side of base, mark the center. Using a drill press, drill a ⅝-inch hole for the tree "trunk." Put small dowels in ascending order, longest to smallest.

If satisfied with the "tree," take it apart to do the painting. Drill a small hole in the wood star and one centered in the top of larger dowel ("tree trunk"). Place a small piece of metal wire, such as from a large paper clip, into star. Check the fit at the top of tree.

3 Spray paint all the dowels with the green paint. Follow precautions on paint can. Place one end of dowels on a small board. Paint star with gold paint. Let them dry a bit and turn them to get all sides. Let them dry overnight or according to manufacturer's instructions, to be thoroughly dry.

Sand entire surface of dowels lightly, sanding through to the wood in some areas. Wipe dowels with a paper towel. Put "tree" together and if dowels fit snugly no gluing is necessary. Put "tree" into base. Finish entire project with a spray acrylic sealer. Let dry.

WINTER-THEME EMBROIDERED SHIRT

Let your holiday- and winter-themed stamps do double duty as the patterns for adding embroidered embellishments to shirts.

To create a new hostess blouse, stamp and hand-stitch your favorite winter-theme images onto strategic areas of a comfortable denim blouse. This is also a great way to make old apparel new again. Just add your own special touches, memories and pet names.

You have all those special winter-theme stamps that you bought to make holiday cards for friends and relatives last year. Now those special favorites can do double duty when you use them to stamp articles of clothing and then hand stitch the image with embroidery floss. The possibilities are endless. You can stamp and stitch your own apparel, or you can create special gifts for other members of your family or friends. Adding your own special touch to a premade garment helps to personalize the gift and shows them that you really care to share a favorite memory. You can also add a name or other special names like "Mom, Best Friend, Holiday Shopper," etc. You probably have just the idea to use for a special gift for a family member or friend.

1 Select coordinating stamps that have a variety of sizes so that you can use different but coordinated images for the right or left front of the blouse, the back shoulder, pocket and the cuffs. Use larger size stamps for the front and medium to small stamps for the shoulder, pocket and cuff of the blouse. Using washable ink that will show up on the denim blouse, stamp the appropriate stamp on the area of the blouse preferred. If you are selecting a stamp that needs a background color, such as a snowman, also stamp the image on a scrap of fabric in the color appropriate for the background color.

2 Cut out a small square of double-sided, fusible fabric to cover the size of the stamped image and using a hot iron, press the fusible fabric on the reverse side of the stamped background fabric. Trim the fabric around the outside of the stamped image and remove the protective fabric from the reverse side of the background. Position the trimmed image on the background fabric directly over the stamped image on the blouse. Ensure that all edges of both images line up. Using a hot iron, press background fabric to the denim blouse. Secure the background fabric to the blouse, using a blanket quilting stitch.

3 With embroidery or quilting needle, and two to four strands of embroidery floss, stitch the remaining image with the satin stitch, backstitch or French knot. The number of strands of floss will depend on the design and how bold an image you want on the apparel. Use satin stitch for bigger areas, the backstitch for outline and the French knot for small areas such as eyes on the image. Multiple French knots can be used in combination for larger areas to give a textured appearance. When stitching is complete, wash the clothing according to manufacturer's instructions to remove any stamping ink that is not covered by the stitching. Press and wear!

Craft Tip

• Select stamps that have a large outline pattern rather than ones that are very detailed. This simplifies the hand stitching and results in more crisp pictures. Select a variety of coordinating stamps and don't be afraid to add a little humor by coordinating images used on the front and back of a blouse. A "before" and "after" image is really cute for this effect. Don't limit yourself to creating personalized apparel for special events and parties. Use stamps and stitching on other items that you want to decorate or personalize such as a canvas bag, a holiday placemat or a wall decoration.

ACCORDION PHOTO ALBUM

Capture grand memories and preserve them in style when you create this wonderful keepsake gift idea.

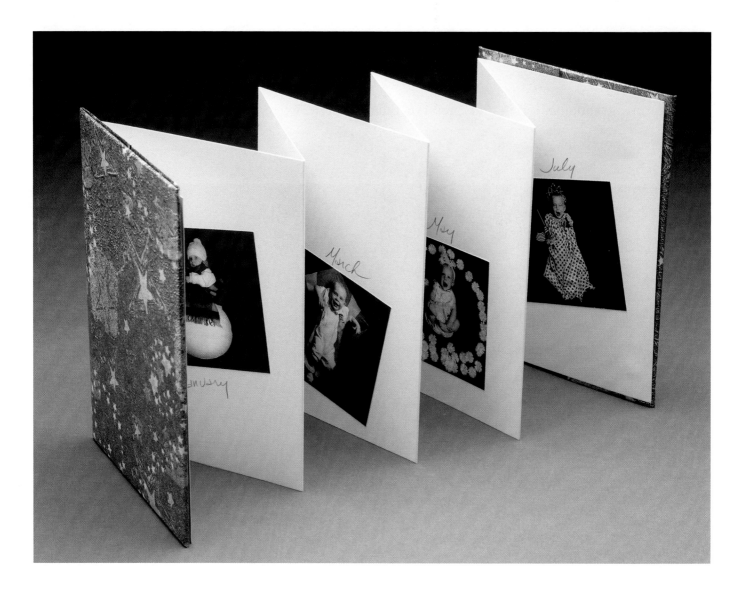

Wrapped up as a holiday gift, unfold the best of memories with this accordion-style photo album. Photographs of the year's events, holidays and everyday activities are given a beautiful three-dimensional display.

Choose a favorite wrapping paper to wrap the front and back of the album cover. Inside, folded paper holds photos on two sides for easy viewing. Color or black-and-white photos design each page. Write your own captions to tell a story, add humor or be a remembrance of events and dates. This album is a special holiday gift that will hold memories for years to come.

Materials & Tools

- 14 photographs; 8 for one side, 6 for reverse side
- 7- by 40-inch piece of heavyweight paper for accordion fold
- Two 5- by 7-inch pieces of cut cardboard
- Two 10- by 14-inch pieces of gift wrap
- Ribbon
- Scissors
- Ruler
- Pencil
- Repositional glue stick
- Creaser or wooden popsicle stick

1 Wrap each 5- by 7-inch cardboard piece in gift wrap. Position cardboard square in middle of 10- by 10½-inch paper, fold over upper then lower edge. Use glue stick to glue under each flap. Now fold over the two remaining sides and glue flaps down.

2 Take the 7- by 40-inch-strip of paper, measure off every 5 inches and draw a light pencil line. Fold first 5 inches, marking forward as if making a gift card. Use a creaser or wooden stick to make a firm crease by starting at top of fold and pressing down entire length of the fold. Take the next 5 inches, marking and folding this backward. Continue to fold forward and backward on all 5-inch markings. You now have a 5- by 7-inch accordion-fold insert. If a 40-inch length of paper is not available, several pieces of shorter paper can be glued together to add up to this length.

3 Glue the top of the accordion insert onto one wrapped end of the 5- by 7-inch gift-wrapped board. Note that the accordion fold will fold open like a book when the front flap is glued down. Take the bottom flap of the accordion insert and glue this down onto the other wrapped end of the 5- by 7-inch gift-wrapped cardboard. Front folded section will hold eight photos, back fold will hold six photos. Glue photos in position on each page or every other page. Add writing, drawings or your own personal touch to each page. Cut a length of ribbon to tie around the album, making it a hidden gift of memories.

Variations

- Use photo corners for positioning photos.
- Personalize front cover with stick-on lettering.
- Add a special photo for front cover.
- Glitter gel pens add a sparkling writing effect.
- Leave back folded sections open for photo additions.

VALENTINE DOOR HANGER

Show them you love them on that very special day, when you make a very special surprise out of this delightful craft project idea.

Here's a fun way to delight a child (or adult) as they wake up on Valentine's morning! Personalize this project for a child by using stickers, or gluing on wooden or plastic animals or sports-themed items. Fill the door hanger with candies, small toys and love notes.

Materials & Tools

- One piece of craft foam
- Approx. 3 yards wide wire ribbon (for handle and sides)
- ½ yard white wire ribbon (for top of handle)
- ¼ yard pink ribbon (for top of handle)
- Approx. 3 yards of ⅛-inch ribbon (for stitching and tails)
- Small roses or flowers of choice (found in the bridal department of craft stores)
- Small, artificial leaves
- Needle with large hole
- Hot glue gun

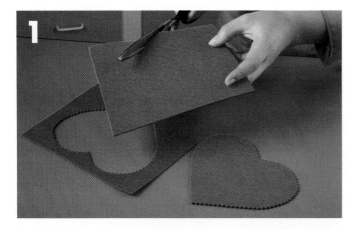

1 Cut out two heart shapes and two side pieces. (Pinking shears were used for this project.)

2 Thread the needle with a 45-inch piece of ⅛-inch ribbon. With wrong sides together and facing out, start sewing the pieces together at the bottom of the heart and the side piece, leaving a long tail of ribbon 6 inches or so) at the bottom. Sew the pieces together with the ribbon, spacing the stitches approximately ½ inch apart. When you reach the top of the side piece, sew three stitches across it, and continue sewing the side piece (from top to bottom) to the other heart piece. At the bottom, leave a long tail of ribbon. Repeat this process on the other side.

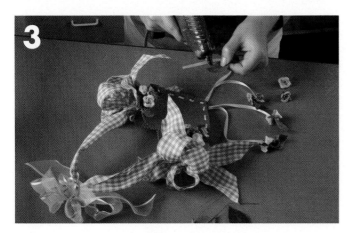

3 To make the handle, cut the wide wired ribbon to the desired length. Run each end of the ribbon through the middle stitch on the side piece, folding it over toward the top, and hot-glue it to secure it. To embellish the hanger, tie a white bow at the top of the ribbon hanger. Hot-glue a smaller pink bow inside the white bow. On the sides, glue down pieces of wire ribbon tails, and wire ribbon loops on the sides. Hot-glue the small flowers on the top sides of the heart. Trim the tail ribbons on the bottom, and hot-glue leaves and flowers on them.

CHRISTMAS STOCKING

Personalize this stocking for most any kid (even if he or she is just a kid at heart!) when you thoughtfully select the fabric for this easy-to-make holiday project.

With the wide variety of novelty fabrics available at fabric stores, you can make a Christmas stocking featuring your child's or grandchild's favorite interest, hobby or dream every year. This project features one of the fun '50s retro fabrics that will be sure to delight your little cowboy or cowgirl.

Materials & Tools

- ½ yard novelty fabric
- ½ yard of Felt (sold by the yard)
- 1 felt square (sold by the piece)
- Approx. 4 yards of thin cording (you can also use twine)
- Trim (optional)

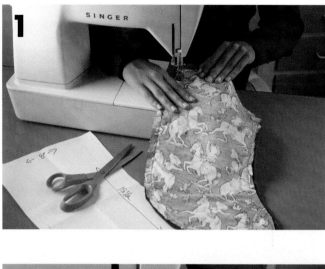

1 Cut out the stocking pattern pieces. With the right sides together, sew the stocking pieces together (½-inch seams). Turn the stocking right side out. Iron the edges.

2 To make the stocking top, cut the felt piece into two pieces measuring 4 inches wide by 9 inches long. Sew ½-inch side seams. Turn the stocking top so that the finished seams are on the outside. Place the stocking top into the inner top edge of the stocking, so that the finished seam of the stocking top meets the inside seam of the stocking. Pin the stocking top into place, matching the side seams. Before sewing, tuck the felt hanger (placed diagonally pointing toward the middle of the stocking) on the upper back corner of the back of the stocking. Sew the stocking top to the stocking. Turn the stocking top over, and iron the edges.

3 To create the name on the stocking top, write out the child's name on a piece of paper, using one continuous line, until you achieve the look you like. Using that as a reference, you can write out the name with white or craft glue, and place the cording down in one continuous line, using pins to anchor it. You can also adhere the cording by simply pinning it in place and whip stitching around the cording.

POLAR FLEECE MITTENS

Don't worry about lost mittens — or cold hands — any more! These polar fleece mittens just can't lose each other.

This project solves the age-old problem of lost mittens. The solution? An updated version of the idea of elastic mitten holders. The project uses a long, narrow piece of polar fleece with each end folded over and sewn together to make mittens. Slide this one long piece of polar fleece into a jacket, and you'll never lose your mittens again! Perfect for kids AND kids at heart!

Materials & Tools

- ½ yard polar fleece (¼ yard for child size)
- Sewing machine

1 Cut the polar fleece into a long strip, about 7 inches wide. (For a child's size, one long piece of polar fleece will probably be enough. For an adult, you will need to cut two pieces, sewing a back middle seam, to get a strip that long.) For either child or adult size, have the recipient stand with their arms pointing straight out horizontally from their sides. Pin the middle of the polar fleece strip to the middle of their back clothing, so it stays in place while you are measuring. From the middle of the back, bring each polar fleece piece to the end of the fingers, and add approximately 9 inches to each end (to fold over to create the mitten). Trim the excess.

2 Fold over the excess and pin at the wrist and where the thumb meets the hand. Add about ½-inch seam allowance to the measurement of the mitten.

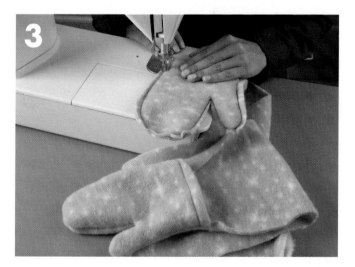

3 Sew the mitten on a sewing machine. (Optional: You can sew a seam across the wrist for added strength. This is shown on the example.) Trim the edges of the mitten to ¼ inch. Turn right side out.

Craft Tip

- Safety-pin the middle back of the polar fleece to the recipient's jacket.

JOURNAL TO A NEW YEAR

Journaling is fun, and important as a way to record and remember events big or small but always meaningful. Here's how to do it in style.

From ancient hieroglyphes to gathered sheets of paper, throughout history people have journaled to mark the passing of time and share ideas from one generation to the next. Journaling can take many forms — a record of daily activities, a place to form ideas and plan future projects, inspiration for an aspiring writer, a memory book for vacations, a gardening logbook and much more. Create your own New Year journal with a few paper products and a creative individual eye. It's a great way to express yourself!

2 After determining how many pages you want to use, cut paper to size of envelope. Hole-punch two holes per page matching placement to envelope cover and back.

1 Place envelope face side down; envelope flap should be facing on your left. Mark two holes 1½ inch from top and bottom on right side, and ½ inch in from the right edge. With paper punch, punch each hole as marked. These will form the cover and back of the journal. The flap on the inside of front and back covers gives you a pocket to add notes, clippings, photos or other special additions to your journal that you would like to keep together with your writing.

3 Assemble cover, pages and back of journal together by matching holes.

Measure elastic cord twice the distance between punched holes. Tie cord into one circle. Insert one loop end into one hole; insert stick into this loop on front cover, pulling cord tight along back side of journal. Insert other loop end of cord into other hole and insert other end of stick. On front cover tie length of ribbon, leaving long ends to use as journal page marker.

HOLIDAY CELEBRATION GLASSWARE

Make your next holiday party extra memorable when you let your guests take home these personalized, handmade treasures.

A handmade gift is always a cherished gift. These elegant, custom-designed glasses make unique and inexpensive party favors for you and guests to take home. A set of four glasses or more makes a wonderful Christmas gift.

You can make your glasses simple or elaborate, personal or general, party specific or just pretty. Draw your own designs freehand, or use a stencil to apply the colors and designs. Add names and dates if you wish.

There are many styles of glasses to choose from, so pick the ones you want to complement the beverages you will be serving. Then use your imagination!

- Glasses
- Delta PermEnamel Glass Paint, your choice of colors and finishes
- Delta PermEnamel Accent Liner
- Delta Air-dry PermEnamel Surface Conditioner
- Stencils (optional)
- Stencil sponges in several sizes
- Paintbrushes
- Palette or paper plate for paints
- Cotton swabs for cleaning small mistakes
- Paper towels

1 Wash the new glasses in warm soapy water so that the surfaces are free from dirt, oils and residue; let them dry. This is an important preparation step.

2 Apply the conditioner called PermEnamel Surface Conditioner to the outside of the glass with a dry, clean paintbrush and let dry thoroughly. Do not rinse or wipe off.

3 Stir the paints well before using. Do not mix water in with the paint. Pour a small amount of paint onto a paper plate or paint palette and use your paintbrush to apply the paint for your own freehand design. For stenciling, carefully tape the stencil to the section of glass you want to paint. Dip your stencil sponge into the paint, blot off excess paint onto the plate or palette and use an up-and-down patting motion to paint the desired area of the stencil. Very carefully move to the next section or color while the paint is still wet so that you can remove your stencil and wash it before it dries. Carefully remove the stencil. Let dry.

4 If you choose to do so, outline designs with PermEnamel Accent Liner after the paint has dried. The size of the hole in the accent liner needle-nose bottle will determine the thickness of your accent lines, so it is best to start off with a small hole and test the size of the line on your plate or pallet. You can always cut a larger hole if needed. Let the accent liner dry. Allow the paint to cure for 10 days before any contact with water or beverages.

WINTER FELT COASTERS

Protect your tables and make them look festive too, when you use these seasonal coasters. They make great take-home party favors too.

Create personalized winter-themed coasters using die-cut felt shapes. Purchase a die-cutter at an arts and crafts store or use one at a local paper crafts store. Create clean professional results with ease.

Seasonal coasters dress up festive holiday drinks. Personalized coasters add a touch of class to your party. Quick and easy yet stylishly fun, you will be sure to enjoy them for years. They also make wonderful gifts for friends or the host of a party. Mix and match different colored felt to create a simple, attractive set.

1 Lay your material between the die-cut pattern and the plastic sheet. Follow instructions for the proper use of the die-cutter. Press the material through. Cut out six patterns in one color and six patterns in a second color to create a set of twelve coasters.

2 Set the circle cutter to cut a circle approximately 3¾ inches. Place the material on top of a self-sealing mat. Center the tool on top of the cut pattern by looking through the clear tool and making sure all edges of the pattern are equally spaced around the circle. Push down using one hand and turn the tool using the other hand. This will score the material for easier cutting. Follow instructions for the circle cutter for proper use. Also cut out six additional circles the same size in one color and six more in the second color. These will become the back of the coasters. Next, cut the circles out using an Xacto knife.

3 Replace the cut pattern in the circle with a pattern cut from the second color. Use the same color as the front of the coaster for the back. Place the two sides of the coaster faced down on top of small blocks. This will keep the front of the coasters clean when spraying. Spray both sides and wait thirty seconds to one minute before putting them together.

Craft Tip

- Die-cutters are great to use for creating professional quality cut patterns.

WINTER

DECORATING

Winter is filled with opportunities for great decorating. There are the holidays, of course, and you'll find plenty of those kinds of ideas here. But winter also lets you work with subtle colors (like blues and whites), and interesting materials (like ice!) to add seasonal beauty to your decorating. Use the time winter offers to the fullest. Then sit back and admire the results.

Facing page: Ice Globe Candle Holders, page 94

OLD-FASHIONED WINDOW WREATH

You might make two or you might make 20. Either way, this old-fashioned window tradition will add light and life to your holiday and winter decorating scheme.

- Foam wreath — 12-inch
- Tinsel garland — about 15 feet
- Plastic electric candle (light candle)
- Duct tape
- Florist's Pins — about 10
- Monofilament
- Hacksaw
- Long-nosed pliers
- 2 by 4 piece of scrap wood
- Thin piece of scrap wood

This beautiful window wreath, complete with electric candle, is reminiscent of years gone by. Hang one wreath in one window, or place one in all the front windows or even all the windows of your home. All winter long or just for the holidays, this wreath creates a warm and welcoming glow.

This project is made with a plastic electric candle placed inside a foam wreath to create the candle effect. Then wrap wreath with tinsel garland. Tinsel garland comes in a variety of colors. Choose a silver or white garland for a wintry sparkling look, or red or burgundy garland for a holiday look. Many other variations are available in garlands, some in old-fashioned combinations such as red and gold. A few strings of miniature lights could be wrapped with the garland, eliminating the center candle.

This is an easy project, with minimal cost. Make larger wreaths for larger windows. The 12-inch wreath shown works well for a typical-sized double-hung or casement window. The wreath could also be hung on an entry door with a window. In this case, the electric cord would need to be taped over to the side of the door, down to the floor and then to an outlet. To always be safe, unplug candle wreaths when not at home and at night when sleeping.

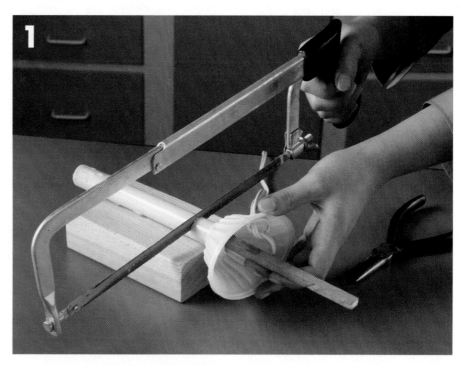

1 Remove the bulb until finished with the project. Place candle part on a 2 by 4 piece of wood to make the candle lie flat for sawing. Place a small scrap of wood inside candle between plastic and electrical cord to prevent cutting through to the cord.

Using a hacksaw, cut the plastic candle to about 5½ inches from the top of the plastic tube to cut line. Turn the candle until the cut is all the way through, keeping the scrap of wood between the plastic and the cord. Cut vertically through the candle stand and cut away the extra part of the tube to remove it from cord. Use long-nose pliers to twist the plastic apart.

2 Using a hacksaw, cut through the foam wreath with one vertical cut. Place the plastic candle in the space, with the bottom of the plastic candle even with the bottom of the wreath. Put small strips of cardboard in front of and behind the candle to fill the space and to hold the candle securely. Wrap duct tape around the candle and wreath to hold them in place. Be sure the candle is securely held in place with duct tape wrapped across the candle and the wreath on front and back. Be sure to cross the bottom of the candle and the wreath a few times.

3 Starting at the bottom of the wreath, secure the wire end of tinsel garland in place with a small piece of duct tape. Wrap garland evenly around the foam wreath, holding garland in place occasionally with a florist's pin. Make sure the entire foam wreath and the duct tape are covered. Secure the end of the tinsel garland with a piece of tape tucked invisibly into the wreath. Make a loop of monofilament and wrap it around the top of the wreath to form a loop for hanging the wreath. Replace the bulb and hang the wreath in a window.

FESTIVE TRIANGULAR LUMINARIAS

What an inviting way to greet guests and let them know they are welcome! These festive luminarias are simple to make, and can be used again and again.

These luminarias with a triangular base are unique. Line them along your front sidewalk on winter evenings when expecting guests, or put them on your front steps. Make them out of tin, which is more reasonable in price, or copper. Add punched holes on all three sides in a snowflake pattern. Snowflakes can be all the same or in varying shapes, as in nature. Other designs good for winter would be stars or candy canes, or for Halloween use bat, ghost or jack-o'-lantern shapes.

The finished size of this luminaria is 9 inches high by 6 inches for each panel. Made smaller, this project could be a votive holder in dimensions such as 4½ inches high, with each panel 4 inches wide.

Purchase tin or sheet metal at a hardware store in 28-gauge weight. A heavier weight would be harder to cut. Or get sheets of tin or copper at a craft store; however, it is more expensive and the largest size is 12 inches by 18 inches. Adapt final dimensions as necessary.

Metal edges are very sharp. Use caution when handling metal edges, or wear leather gloves and tape sharp edges with masking tape. Also, wear glasses or safety glasses when cutting metal and wood as a precautionary measure.

Since most people want more than one luminaria, it is easier and more time efficient to create at least four. One project takes about 1½ hours, but creating four at the same time, in an assembly line process, is faster, taking about 3 hours.

Craft Tip

- When cutting long lines, turn the project around about halfway through and cut from the other side. This avoids problems with the last cut wanting to bend instead of cut. Remember to wear leather gloves and glasses when cutting metal.

Materials & Tools

- Sheet metal — tin or copper — 28 gauge, at least 19 inches by 10 inches (for four, at least a 30-inch-square piece)
- 1 by 6 piece of scrap wood (to make a 6⅜-inch equilateral triangle)
- Candle and holder — 8 inches by 2-inch diameter
- Wire — fine gauge — a few feet
- Snowflake pattern or stencil about 3½ inches in diameter
- Six carpet tacks — about 3½ inches
- Radial arm or miter saw
- Awl or nail
- Hammer
- Tin snips
- Rubber or leather mallet
- Masking tape
- Square

1 Mark a 9½- by 18½-inch rectangle on the back of the metal with a felt-tip marker. If making four luminarias, mark all at the same time, to make sure they fit and take advantage of the cutting lines. Cut at marked lines.

Place masking tape on all cut edges to prevent getting cut. Turn piece over and score with a sharp edge, like the cutting edge of the tin snips, the following fold lines: On one short edge, score a line ½ inch in; on one long edge (this will be the top) score ½ inch in from edge; on the 9½-inch direction, score a line 6 inches from nonscored edge and 12 inches (this should make three 6- by 9-inch sections). See photo. Also cut away the ½-inch square formed by the scored lines near the two edges. Also cut a "V" at the top edge where vertical fold lines cross horizontal fold lines.

2 Center the snowflake pattern or stencil in the top half of the section between score lines and tape. Place a piece of scrap wood under the area to be punched. Use an awl or nail and hammer to punch the holes. Punch where there are points in the design and where there are obvious indentations or curves. Punch all designs and hold up to light to check that all punches have gone through.

At bottom edge (the one edge without fold line) punch 2 holes 2 inches apart and 2 inches from scored edges. Also punch 3 sets of double holes ½ inch apart on both short edges. The holes should be about ¼ inch in from edge and start at ½ inch from top and bottom. It is easier to make a cardboard template to make these exact as they will need to line up for the last step.

3 To fold metal, place edge to be folded on a sharp, sturdy edge, such as a table saw or workbench. Scored line should be placed exactly at edge of surface. Do the long edge (top) first. Using the mallet, hit the edge in a downward motion. Then turn the metal over and gently pound the edges flat. Then do the short edge, leaving it at about a 90-degree angle. For the remaining folds, you may be able to use your hands to make the fold. This will avoid any damage on the right side of the project. Make the metal into the shape of a triangle. Overlap the folded edge, to cover cut edge. Hold it with a rubber band. Using wire and starting at the top, thread it through the holes from the inside. Twist the wire after each set of holes.

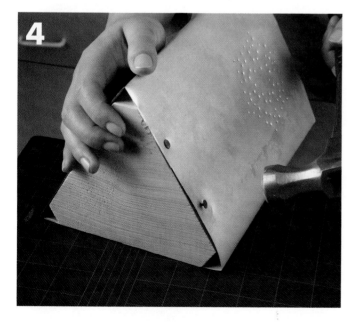

4 Cut a 6⅜-inch equilateral triangle from a scrap of 1 by 6 wood. Cut ½ inch off each point of the triangle. Place in bottom of luminaria and using the holes already punched, tack in place with a hammer. Make sure that the metal does not extend beyond the wood base so it will protect the sharp edge. If making votives, metal can be washed in mild soapy water to remove fingerprints and after thoroughly dried, can be sprayed with a clear acrylic sealer.

WINTER DECOUPAGE PICTURE FRAME

Whether you use it to decorate your own home or give it as a gift to someone special, you know this personalized frame is going to be appreciated.

Use wrapping or tissue paper to make this one-of-a-kind picture frame. Add wooden shapes to create a scene or use wrapping paper with the shapes already part of the design. The design shown here is winter related, however it may be holiday related or may have a leisure activity theme that is enjoyed by the family, such as skiing or the family pet. The wooden shapes can be extended from the frame, creating dimension. The wooden shapes, such as the birdhouse, also give it more dimension. The wooden shapes can be painted or done in decoupage; however, the thin wooden shapes may warp from the decoupage medium.

Materials & Tools

- Wooden craft picture frame — at least 8 inches square, with a frame surface of 2½ inches
- Tissue paper in red, white and shades of blue and green or wrapping paper, as desired
- Decoupage medium
- Wooden shapes — thin: stars — 1½ inch; mini birds — 1³/₁₆ by ⅝ inch; folk art trees — 2¼ inches; larger tree — 5 inches.
- Wooden shape — thick; birdhouse — 1½ inches
- Acrylic craft paint — white, yellow, gold (red and green — if not using decoupage for wooden shapes)
- Small twig
- Paintbrush
- Glue gun
- Sandpaper

1 Remove glass from picture frame. Determine design by laying wooden shapes on frame and also deciding on placement of background. Sketch lightly with a pencil the desired horizon line between the sky and the snow. To avoid having to use many layers of white tissue paper, paint the area to be covered with white tissue paper (snow) with a coat or two of white craft acrylic paint. Also paint the top of the birdhouse with white paint. Let dry.

Cut the first layers of tissue paper from the lighter blue to follow the horizon line. Do this in two sections, working around frame opening and letting the tissue paper overlap each section and overlap the edges, leaving enough to go around to the back of frame.

Start to decoupage by spreading the decoupage medium on the frame, in the desired design area, and placing the

tissue paper over it. Cut the next layer of tissue of a shade darker, and do the same. Put decoupage medium both under each layer and on top of each layer. Continue with as many layers as desired. When completed, let dry. When dry, clip into the corners on the inside of the frame and, with decoupage medium, pull the tissue around frame to back of frame. Do the same on the outside of the frame and let dry. While this is drying, go to Step 2 and prepare the wooden shapes. Make sure paintbrush is completely clean before starting to use the white tissue paper. When the sky decoupage section is completely dry, do the entire decoupage process for the snow, using the white tissue paper. Layering it in the same way that the sky was layered will give the snow more dimension. Decoupage white tissue on the top of the birdhouse also. Let dry. Go to Step 3.

2 Paint the stars with two coats of yellow paint. Let dry between coats. Paint or decoupage the other shapes. The birds will require two layers of red tissue and the trees can be done using two to three shades of green tissue for more dimension. Let dry. When dry, the excess tissue can be pulled off these shapes, leaving a ragged edge. If painting the birds and trees, use one to two coats of paint. Let the coats dry between. Add a yellow beak to the birds, with a dot of yellow paint. When stars are dry, add a coat of metallic gold for a bit of shimmer. Let all shapes dry. Go back to Step 1 and decoupage the snow.

3 After all the decoupage is entirely dry, which may take overnight, sand the back edges of the frame to cleanly make an edge and pull any remaining tissue off back of frame. Finalize placement of all shapes, including twig for "holding" the birdhouse. Using glue gun, glue all shapes in place. Let dry. Put glass back into the frame.

Craft Tip

- Caution: Colored tissue paper will bleed so use rubber gloves and also avoid getting darker colors on lighter surface.

SNOWMAN PAINTED BOX

It takes a little while for the paint to dry, but otherwise this folksy box is a quick-and-easy

breeze to make.

This picture frame box is painted to look worn, and the designs created to resemble folk art. Choose colors with this in mind. The designs are easy to do, even for the inexperienced painter. A combination of sponging, free-hand and spattering create the folk art look. Paint a piece of scrap pine board in the background color to use for practicing designs. Since these designs are folk art, perfection is not necessary. Details are drawn in with a paint pen. Additional details of wood feet and a knob for the top create the finished look.

Add additional details if you wish. Add a medium to dark stain to edges with exposed wood and wipe off immediately, for a different look. Two small rectangular pieces of leather can be attached with tacks to cover the hinges. You could also put another piece of leather on the front of the cover to resemble a latch. The top of the box can be left plain, or can be spattered.

This project takes about 5 hours, but most of that is drying time between coats and design elements. That gives you time to get some other projects going!

Materials & Tools

- Wooden craft box with a front design surface of about 3 inches high by 6 inches wide
- Acrylic craft paint in off-white, orange, forest/hunter green, black
- Teal blue latex or spray paint
- Black paint pen
- Spray matte acrylic sealer
- Five ¾-inch-round knob head
- Expandable sponge for sponge painting
- Small round paintbrush
- Sandpaper
- Paper plate
- Scrap of pine board
- Old toothbrush
- Wood glue or glue gun

1 Remove hinges or any hardware, if possible, otherwise cover them with masking tape. Many of the craft boxes have hinges and details that can not be removed. Paint entire box, wood knobs for feet and front handle at this time. Let dry according to the manufacturer's instructions. Sand edges to remove paint to let wood show through. Lightly sand all surfaces in direction of grain and wipe with paper towel. Run sandpaper over knobs and, in areas, sand through to the wood. Knobs can also be left natural.

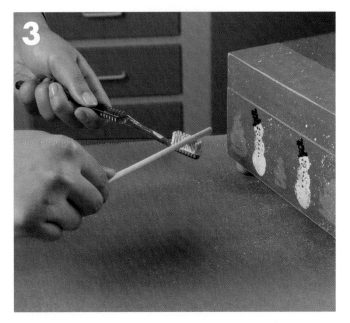

2 For the snowmen, cut three circles, about $\frac{7}{8}$-inch, $\frac{5}{8}$-inch, $\frac{7}{16}$-inch, from expandable sponge. Also cut a narrow wedge shape for carrot nose and a rectangle, about $\frac{1}{2}$ inch by $\frac{1}{4}$ inch, for hat. Expand sponges with water and let them dry a bit. For the snowman, start with bottom snowball using largest sponge circle and off-white paint. Sponge with a firm touch, using largest to smallest circles, overlapping them a bit. Let dry. Immediately wipe off any mistakes with a damp paper towel. Let snowman dry completely before adding details.

Use rectangular sponge with black paint for hat, drawing in brim with brush. Add dots for eyes, mouth and buttons, with black paint pen. Using narrow wedge of sponge and orange paint, add the carrot nose. For the trees, turn board (box) upside down. Starting from bottom and widest part of tree, using green paint, loosely zigzag brush toward you, narrowing design to nothing. Decide on placement of designs on box. Paint box with designs, as on practice board.

3 Practice applying snow on painted practice board. Use an old toothbrush dabbed in a small amount of off-white paint and run a small dowel or chopstick across it a few inches above the surface to be spattered. Only do a couple of passes with the dowel before removing paint buildup on dowel. Tape top of box to prevent it from getting spattered, if desired.

When efficient with the spatter technique, spatter box where desired. Uncover hinges or put them on if they were removed. Apply wood knobs to bottom of box for feet with glue gun or wood glue and to front top of lid for handle. Or cover hinges with leather rectangles and tacks and on front lid, apply a leather rectangle with two tacks at top, to resemble a latch, if desired. Let glue dry. Spray with matte acrylic sealer over entire box. Let dry according to manufacturer's instructions.

Craft Tip

- Spray paint is the fastest and will need two to three coats, because coats of spray should not be heavy. If using paint and brush, two coats should cover well. Paintbrush lines should go in one direction and with the grain. Remember to paint a piece of scrap board for practice.

POLAR FLEECE VALANCE OR SHELF

Create a shelf for holiday displays of all kinds. Gear the fabric's color and theme to the room. This shelf is easy to create and mount.

A simple wood shelf — perfect for mounting over a window — can be covered with a wintry, Northwood's printed polar fleece. You can also use this shelf for displaying lightweight mementos or collections such as stuffed toys or framed pictures. The polar fleece does not require any sewing, as it will not fray, so this project is ideal for a non-sewer. The fabric valance can be easily removed and changed as the seasons change or to create a different look in the room. Other pattern ideas include NFL, NBA, NHL or racing logos for a sporting theme, or one of the many theme-printed polar fleeces available.

Some prints are directional and that determines the way that it is cut and the amount of fabric to purchase. The polar fleece valance shown has a design that runs lengthwise and the amount that would need to be purchased is equal to the full length of the shelf plus the overhang on both

ends. If the design runs crosswise or has no design direction, the valance can be cut crosswise and the amount needed would be the depth of the valance, unless the length of valance plus overhang is more than the 60-inch width of the fabric. Then the amount of fabric needed would be 2 times the depth. This project above is 37½ inches wide, with an overhang on both sides of about 6 inches. The dimensions for the above will be given in the instruc-

tions; however, you will be able to adapt for any size window or shelf.

Variations on this project include a double layer of fabric, with one layer longer than the other and made from a polar fleece of contrasting color. The front of the valance may be at an angle and the double layer with the angle going the opposite way.

Materials & Tools

- Polar Fleece — for amount see above
- Pine board — 1 inch by 6 inches by 4 feet (if valance is to be larger than the one shown, a longer board will be needed)
- 3-inch angle irons — 2 (if the shelf will be longer than 60 inches, an angle iron for the middle will be needed)
- 4 wood screws — about 1½ inches long (plus anchors if needed for wall)
- Electric drill
- Shears or rotary cutter
- Buttons or other trim at ends of valance

1 Measure window from outside edge of side molding to other outside edge of molding. Add at least 2¼ inches for each side (total of 4½ inches). This will allow for the angle iron to be placed between inside edge of valance and window molding. Cut board to 37½ inches or desired measurement. For sides of wooden valance cut two pieces, each 5¼ inches. Place each side vertically under each end of board. Make all edges flush. Drill two holes ⅜ inch in from end of board and into side pieces. Put in screw. Repeat for other end of board.

2 Turn wooden valance upside down and measure ¾ inch in from side piece. Place angle iron on that mark and even with back edge of board. Mark holes. Do the same for the other end. Put up to window to check placement of angle irons. Drill holes and put in screws. Measure valance from bottom edge of side piece, over top and to bottom of other side piece. For the above project, this is 49½ inches.

3 Place fabric on large cutting surface and mark the length. Remember that if the design has a directional pattern take that into account when marking this distance. Measure the depth of valance from back edge of top board forward and have at least a 6-inch drop. This should be 11½ inches. Mark this distance. With a marking pencil, mark the rectangle that these measurements form. Smoothly cut the rectangular piece of fabric. Place fabric on wooden valance to check length and width. Trim any extra length of fabric at this time.

Mount the board, placing it on top of the window molding, centering it and marking placement for screws. Drill hole in wall. If anchors are needed make the hole the appropriate size. Put board in place and put in screws. Place polar fleece over wooden valance, centering it and putting it flush with wall.

Smooth it. Because the polar fleece has texture it should hold in place; however, thumbtacks can be added near the back wall to hold it in place. The fabric over the side can be folded to make a square corner and secured or the polar fleece can be left to drape freely. If creating a square corner, hold the fold in place temporarily with a pin and trim any excess fabric created by the fold. A decorative pin, button or other decorative item can be placed to hold the fold on each end.

ELEGANT NEW YEAR'S DRIED ARRANGEMENT

Who needs flowers to create an attractive arrangement? Not you!

Use tall, slender and willowy dried stems to make this arrangement. It is made elegant and festive with white and silver spray paint, and a touch of glitter. Put the arrangement in a glass, jar, special vase or other unique container. If the container is glass, fill it with marbles or stones to hold the arrangement in place and create an elegant and attractive appearance.

This arrangement is about 36 inches high. Place it on a mantel, sideboard or endtable. This arrangement can also be adapted to other holidays such as Valentine's Day or Easter.

In an arrangement like this, less is better. Purchase one dominant stem such as curly willow for the focal point. Select two other types of stems. You can also use willow stems and other dried stems you may find in nature. The cost of this project will vary depending on the cost of the container and the stems selected.

1 Determine stem selection and approximate placement of stems for arrangement while in container. Select one prominent stem, taller and with more interest than the others. All others should be shorter than this stem. Fill in with straight stems and one leafy, yet slender stem. Cut extra length off the bottom of stems. Decide which are to be painted white, silver or a combination. Glitter or iridescent paint can also be strategically used. Spray-paint all stems with one or two coats of white to completely cover. Hold the stems and turn while spraying, and place in a container to dry.

To tip the leaves with silver, prop up the stem facing you and spray. Also you may wish to spray-paint some of the narrow stems silver. Good places to use glitter are at tips of leaves or the top of the curly willow. Use a brush to apply glue and then the glitter in order to control its placement. Allow the painted stems a few hours for final drying, even when using quick-dry spray paint.

Materials & Tools

- Tall, straight dried stems, such as willow, curly willow, bamboo, bearded wheat or tall grasses, about 36 inches high
- Leafy tall dried stem, such as myrtle
- Glass vase or other container — tall and narrow (wide enough for your hand to go in)
- Spray paint — fast-dry, gloss — white and silver
- Glue and fine glitter or glitter paint (optional)
- Wired sheer ribbon — 1 inch wide and about 3 yards
- Crystal garland — a few yards
- Glass marbles — enough to fill the container
- Dry florist's foam — a small piece
- Rubber bands
- Wire cutters

2 Prepare the container by cutting the dry florist's foam about 2 inches thick and 1½ inches smaller than the inside of the container, leaving enough room for the marbles to completely surround the foam. Using a glue gun, center and secure the foam to the bottom of the container. Let dry briefly.

Put marbles into container to the top of the foam. Arrange stems as desired and secure the bundle tightly with 2 rubber bands or twist-ties. When happy with the basic arrangement, place it into the container and securely into the foam. Holding the arrangement with one hand, add marbles to the container. Work with the arrangement in doing this to ensure that it is centered and arranged as desired.

3 Double the piece of ribbon and place it around the top of the container and tie a bow, arranging it as desired. If the vase will not hold a bow securely, tie the bow around the bundle where it meets the top of the vase. Drape crystal garland through the arrangement and down the side of the vase. This can also separate some of the stems and hold them in place.

WIRE MESH HANGING HEART

Make a three-dimensional mesh heart to fill with dried rosebuds and petals, or some other kind of fragrant and pretty potpourri. Hang it on a wall or give it as a gift.

Trim this heart for a country look or a more elegant look. You can hang it as an ornament and view it from both sides. For this, wrap both sides of the heart "box" with ribbon. Use a 1-inch cloth woven ribbon, as a satin one may catch on the wire and snag. The base of this project is hardware cloth. The ½- and ¼-inch mesh works best.

Materials & Tools

- Hardware cloth — a 12-inch by 14-inch piece
- 1-inch woven ribbon — about 4 yards
- Wire, fine gauge — a few feet
- Dried rosebuds and petals or potpourri
- Other embellishments, such as flowers, greens or other ribbons
- Wire cutter
- Long-nosed pliers
- Leather gloves

1 Make and cut out a heart-shaped pattern measuring about 7 inches wide by about 7 inches high. Place the pattern on the hardware cloth. Make sure that the heart-shaped pattern is centered so that a vertical wire is at the center and trace two heart shapes on hardware cloth using a wide felt-tipped pen. Cut both heart shapes from the hardware cloth using wire cutters. Also cut two rectangular shapes, 2 inches by 12 inches, leaving one long side on each with the wires extending. The other long side should be smooth. Place the narrow ends of rectangles together and wire one set of ends together. Separate the other ends. Near the wired part, hold the side pieces upright and wrap each side around a cup, creating a gentle curve to start the heart shape of the side pieces of the "box."

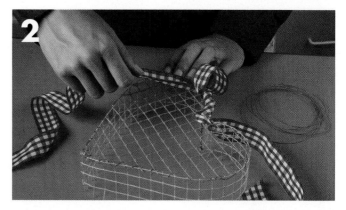

2 Place one of the heart shapes on top of the side pieces, with smooth edges of rectangular pieces facing up. Work the shapes together. Start wrapping the edges with wire from the top center of the heart shape. Secure the beginning of the wire well. Wrap the other side of the heart with wire in the same manner. At the heart bottom or point, cut any excess hardware cloth from the side pieces. Wrap the wire along the point from heart-shaped piece to the back side of the "box." Next, wrap with the ribbon starting at top center of heart shape and leaving about 10 to 12 inches of extra ribbon. The goal is to cover the edges of the heart, but it does not need to be smooth and even. Wrap to the point and leave the extra ribbon. Do the same on the other side.

3 Turn the "box" over and add rosebuds and petals or potpourri. Place the remaining heart-shaped wire piece on top, working it into place. Turn the protruding wires around the heart-shaped wire piece with pliers to secure. Tie the top ribbons forming a loop for hanging. Embellish as desired with dried flower blossoms or greens such as ivy, at the top of the heart or by hanging more ribbons or other elements such as beads, at the bottom of the heart.

ICE GLOBE CANDLE HOLDERS

It's winter, so you might as well add ice to your decorating for a special occasion. This project is fun to do — and the results look almost magical!

This project combines fire and ice for unique and magical candle holders. Use these candle holders outdoors as luminaries up your walkway, or in a grouping near your front door. You could also use as centerpieces right on your table; just watch out for the "melt factor!"

Craft Tip

- Freezing times will vary so you may need to experiment as to how long to keep the balloons in the freezer. For this project, I kept the small globes in the freezer for 9 hours, and the large globes for 11 hours.

Materials & Tools

- Helium quality balloons, 7 inch for the smaller globes, 12 inch for the larger globes
- Water
- Bowls and washcloths
- Saucepan with a couple of inches of water
- Teaspoons
- Tea lights
- Long matches or hand-held lighter
- Freezer space (If conditions are right, freeze them outside)

1 Fill the balloons with water to the desired size of ice globe. Line the bowl with a wash-cloth to hold it in place. Set the balloon, top side down, in the bowl. Put it in the freezer.

To check readiness, remove the balloon/bowl from the freezer, pierce the balloon and remove it. You can determine the approximate width of the ice visually. They are better thicker than thinner.

2 If the walls of the ice globe appear about ½ inch thick, gently begin chipping away at the very top of the ice globe with an ice pick or an awl until you have a small hole. With a towel, pick up the ice globe and empty all the excess water out of it.

3 Keep in the freezer until you plan to use the ice globe. Drop a tea light into it and light it, using a long matchstick or a handheld lighter.

When using the ice globes indoors, place them in saucers or platters, surrounded by fresh or silk holly, flowers or evergreen branches. As always, use these ice globe candle holders under adult supervision, and use extra caution when children are present.

SNOWMAN NAPKIN HOLDERS

Make your holiday table happy and colorful with these fun-loving napkin holders.

This is a project everyone will enjoy — adults and kids alike. If you haven't tried any of the polymer clays yet, this simple project will inspire you. Other ideas for napkin holders include gingerbread men, a Santa face, Rudolf, and large candy canes.

Materials & Tools

- Sculpey clay (white, yellow, red, blue)
- Wooden napkin holder (available at craft stores)
- Aluminum foil
- Twigs
- Disposable knife
- Toothpicks
- Black permanent Sharpie marker
- Baby oil

1 Cut the blue clay into small pieces and cover the entire surface of the wooden napkin holder, smoothing out air bubbles and wrinkles. The warmth of your hands will make the clay more pliable. You can add little white balls and flatten them in securely to the blue surface to create a polka-dot effect. Clean hands and fingers between each color with baby oil.

2 To create the snowman body, roll up aluminum foil into 3 balls, small, medium and large. Press each aluminum ball quite hard onto a table top to create a flat bottom for easier stacking. Cut the white clay into small pieces and completely cover the aluminum foil balls, until they are smooth. Roughen each of the joining surfaces a bit with a toothpick, and place each one on top of the other, using a toothpick around the edges to also help the clay surfaces adhere.

3 To create the green hat, mix a little blue/yellow clay together. For the carrot nose, mix a little red/yellow together. (This is a good opportunity to teach younger children the idea of mixing primary colors to create secondary colors.) For the striped scarf, make 2 thin "snakes" of red and yellow, twist together and flatten. Cut to size.

4 Using the toothpick, poke a hole in the snowman body for each twig arm. Insert each twig and push white clay around the twig to secure it. Make mittens and a snowball for the snowman, pressing them onto the ends of the twigs. Also place some snowballs at the base of the snowman.

To attach the snowman to the napkin holder, roughen each of the surfaces a bit with a toothpick, and then press into each other. Also use a toothpick around the edges to press the clay into each surface to adhere to the other. Bake in the oven set on a piece of tinfoil on a baking sheet according to instructions on the package. With the Sharpie marker, add eyes and a great big smile.

ARTISTIC SHADES

Winter is short enough on light the way it is. So let this artistic shade give you privacy while maximizing the amount of daylight reaching any room in your house.

This window project takes few materials but has a big visual impact on your home. Start with a beautiful handmade paper available at craft and paper stores. Choose from floral, abstract or geometric designs, whatever ties best to your own home decor. The more transparent the paper, the more light will come through. Vellum papers are also available; they have a transparent quality with a visual design overlay.

Cut or collage together a variety of shapes and sizes to make one shade piece. As window sizes vary, cut paper in sections and layer them to cover all or only a portion of a window. Try a seasonal change to your papers; pastels for spring and summer, primary colors in fall and winter.

Here's one other idea: Incorporate the written word onto your papers. Write a verse, copy a favorite poem, or let your own writing become the design. Then let this artistic paper shade hang from your window, letting natural light illuminate your creativity.

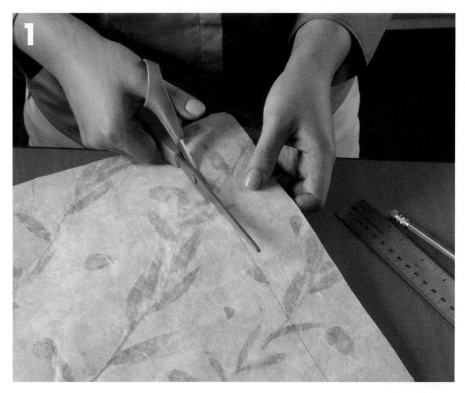

1 Take spring tension rod and expand to width of window, test by placing inside window frame to make tight and even contact. Size paper to fit window width. Determine measurement of paper length by measuring from rod to finished length. Cut paper with scissors to height and width measurements.

Materials & Tools

- Raffia ribbon
- Handmade paper, or vellum sheets
- Expandable spring tension rod
- Scissors
- Pencil
- Paper punch

Craft Tips

- More than one rod can be placed in window, papers can overlap each other to add more interest.
- Use in door windows as well, mounting with double-stick tape to frame of window.
- Can easily be moved for cleaning or to change an arrangement.
- Try a cafe curtain rod if you would like to permanently mount the shade to the window frame.
- Recover an old lamp shade, by taking off its shade, tracing the shape onto paper and cutting to size.
- Suspend a framed piece of paper in your window for a colorful window accent.

2 Determine top and bottom of paper by design pattern. With pencil mark the top edge of paper, measuring every 3 inches across and ½ inch down. Make holes on each mark by using paper punch.

3 Measure length of raffia ribbon that will cover the length of paper, plus extra for tying up the ends. Carefully lace ribbon in and out of holes, joining paper to rod. Use extra ribbon on ends to tie a nonslip knot, leaving extra length if adding a bow finish. Paper will fall evenly after it has had some time to hang from the rod.

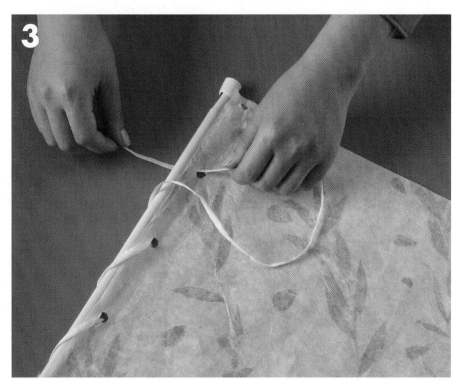

WINTER

GARDENING

Just because it's winter doesn't mean you have to leave your love of gardening behind. You can grow plants indoors — like the herb garden described here — or stick with traditional houseplants. You can "push spring" a little bit and use bulbs to create glorious, colorful blooms inside. And you can plan now for all of summer's gardening endeavors, some of which will add life to your outdoor garden next winter!

Facing page: Bouquet Garden, page 129

WINDOWSILL HERB GARDEN

Grow a kitchen herb garden indoors for the winter. You'll love growing something fresh

and green. And you'll love the wonderful tastes the herbs bring to your cooking.

During the growing season, most home gardeners make more than ample use of their herb gardens. A snip of rosemary here, a pinch of mint there — you can count on herbs to restore gusto to bland food or to take the place of salt or fat in a health-conscious recipe.

But then comes winter, when most herb gardens are covered with snow. Dried herbs in tiny but expensive jars are just not the same. Frozen herbs do a little better job of enhancing flavor, but they still pale next to the taste of fresh. That's why, each winter, it's great to make plans to bring an herb garden inside!

Dill, parsley, and celeriac all do well when grown on a sunny windowsill.

All container plants — especially house-grown herbs — are completely dependent on the gardener for water and food.

*Culinary bay (*Laurus nobilis*) thrives indoors in most conditions.*

Choosing What Herbs to Grow

Before we get started, lets cover what you can and can't expect from a windowsill herb garden. A windowsill garden will provide some fresh herbs to spark up a salad, or add zip to a soup or stew, but don't expect the same abundant pickings you'd get from herbs in your summer garden. Most herbs do grow well inside, but even when tucked into sunny windows, the plants will grow more slowly than they do outside because there is less daylight, and they are confined to a pot.

Herbs are divided into two broad groups, annuals and perennials. For winter windowsill gardens, the annual herbs — basil, cilantro, dill, parsley (actually a biennial) and fennel — are best started from seed. If you want to grow perennial herbs in the house, such as rosemary, tarragon, lemon balm, sage, thyme, oregano and bay, you're better off potting up nursery-grown plants or digging these from your outdoor garden and moving them inside when it gets cold.

Perennials can be started from seed but they won't grow big enough for you to harvest much from them during the winter months. One exception might be chives, which are fast growers. But these mild onion-family members can also be dug up from the garden and potted for indoor use.

Potting Herbs Is Easy

Use both clay and plastic pots for windowsill gardens — the choice is really up to you. Keep in mind that clay pots are porous and will dry out sooner than plastic ones will, so you'll have to water these more frequently.

No matter how good your garden soil is, don't use it for starting your pot-grown herbs. And don't use packaged potting soil. Both of these compact too tightly, which hampers drainage and root develop-

A sunny window is a wonderful spot for herbs.

Clear bags or plastic containers trap humidity and help germination.

ment. Instead, use commercially prepared sterile soil mixes, sold under brand names such as Pro-Mix, Jiffy-Mix, Hoffman or Terralite. (If you can't find these brands, ask your local nursery for a good seed-starting mixture.)

All of these mixes contain varying proportions of peat, vermiculite, perlite and some nutrients.

These mixes are bone-dry and dusty, and need to be moistened before use. Save a couple of steps and some cleanup by cutting a slit in the bag and adding just enough water to dampen the mix. (You don't want it wringing wet.) Then scoop this dampened mix into 5- to 8-inch pots. Use these larger pots so that you won't need to transplant young seedlings later on.

Sprinkle a generous pinch of seeds on the surface of your pot, barely cover them with a bigger pinch of the soil mix, and then gently press down with your fist to put the seed into good contact with the soil. No further watering is necessary. Place the pot in a plastic bag, seal with a twist-tie and then place the pot where it will get bottom heat. Some people put their pots on the top of their cellar furnace, or on top of the refrigerator. You want the pots to be in an area where the temperature is about 70°F.

Seeds should germinate in three to seven days; parsley and fennel may take longer. As soon as the seeds sprout, remove the plastic bag and move the pot to a warm, light location without direct sun.

In about 10 days, move the pot to bright sunlight. The more sun the plants get, the better they will grow. Move some of your herbs from room to room during the day to extend their time in the sun.

You'll find that some of your seedlings will be crowded in their pots. Don't thin dill, fennel (grown for its ferny leaves), cilantro or chives, but transplant both basil and parsley seedlings to one or two plants per pot. If you don't want to thin your basil or parsley, that's fine. They'll do fine tightly clustered in their pots.

Bringing Outside Herbs In

Some perennial herbs are so tough they can over-winter outdoors in most climates: sage, thyme, chives, oregano, lemon balm, tarragon and winter savory are a few that do fine in Zone 6 or milder. However, you do have to dig up three tender perennials — rosemary, bay and lemon grass — and bring them indoors to join the houseplants in a sunny room. (In the South and West, rosemary and bay live through most winters. Only in the tropics can lemon grass stay outdoors.)

Each fall, dig around the periphery of the herbs you want to bring inside, looking for plants with low-growing branches that have rooted, or for isolated clumps within clumps that you can separate from the mother plants. Then pot these in your seed-starting mixture, fortify them with a pinch of time-release fertilizer such as Osmocote or Sta-green, and prune them back by at least a third. Leave these pots outdoors on a shady porch for a few weeks to get

For a touch of the tropics, pot up some heat-loving lemongrass and grow it inside. Rosemary is another popular perennial that will live year-round in warm climates.

How To
Getting Seedlings Started

As winter nears, and certainly as it progresses, most plant markets and nurseries have sold out of last year's seed supply and have not yet received a fresh shipment for next spring. So you may want to order your seeds from a garden catalog.

But you probably still have some leftover seeds from this past spring that were never planted. It's fine to use up these old seeds if they're still fresh.

Check the date on the package; if your seeds are more than two years old, order a fresh supply.

You can easily check whether old seeds are still viable. Place 10 seeds about an inch apart on a double thickness of dampened paper towel. Roll the towel up like a jelly roll, twist the ends, and then place the roll in a plastic bag to trap moisture. Seal the plastic bag with a twist-tie, and move it to a warm place to facilitate germination. (The top of a refrigerator is a good option.)

In three to five days, open the bundle. If you don't see any sign of germination, rewrap and check again three days later. At this point, if all seeds have sprouted, you know you have good seeds. If only half your seeds have sprouted, the seeds are still usable, but you'll have to plant twice as many to get the amount of plants you want. If less than half your seeds have sprouted, throw them away and buy new ones.

1 It's easy to check seed viability and the germination rate with the "wet towel" test.

2 Place seeds on any good seed-starting mix, cover with a pinch of soil, and press down.

3 Place the planting container in a plastic bag to trap moisture. Place in a warm spot.

4 Move pot to a sunny area. Herbs such as the cilantro above won't need thinning.

them acclimated to their potted homes. If you intend to overwinter nursery-bought perennial seedlings, repot them in 6-inch pots in seed-starting mix.

Before bringing any garden-grown herb indoors, hose it off with a vigorous stream of water. This gets rid of bugs that might be lurking in the foliage.

Here's a potting tip from Rose Marie Nichols-McGee of Nichols Garden Nursery in Albany, Oregon. She recommends potting up tarragon before the ground freezes, but leaving the pot outside for about a month, until it has experienced several freezes.

Tarragon evidently needs this period of dormant cold to complete its growth cycle. After the month is over, bring your tarragon indoors, and, thinking spring has arrived, it will start growing again.

Fertilize and Water

Plants in an outdoor garden can generally struggle along and survive (sort of) even if their gardener forgets to water or fertilize. That's not the case with indoor plants. Plants in pots are totally dependent on you for their life, and they'll die if you neglect them.

Potted plants dry out more rapidly inside a heated house. Use the fingertip test before watering: stick your index finger into the soil about to the first knuckle. If the soil is dry at that point, it's time to water. Water and fertilize at the same time using a

Why not an informal herb centerpiece at your next dinner party? (Add a name tag to a small pot and you have both a party favor and a placecard.)

water-soluble fertilizer such as Miracle-Gro or Schultz, diluted to half strength. If the label says to use 1 tablespoon to a gallon, make your mixture with only half a tablespoon.

Many herbs like similar conditions, and could be grown together.

Recipe
Herbed Pasta

1 lb. pasta, preferably thin spaghetti

1 cup of mixed herbs (¼ parsley, ¼ rosemary, ¼ basil and ¼ of any others that are available, such as thyme or savory. Actually, the variety and quantity is flexible, but mixing at least 4 herbs is important for a blended taste.)

½ cup extra-virgin olive oil

⅛ teaspoon salt

⅛ teaspoon freshly ground pepper

1 While pasta is cooking, chop herbs. Sprinkle herbs in bottom of serving bowl. Heat olive oil. As soon as oil starts to smoke, remove from heat and pour over herbs. Drain pasta; place in serving bowl. Toss with oil and herbs; add salt and pepper to taste. Serve.

A word of caution: Don't overwater! More house-plants (and that's what your potted herbs are) perish from too much watering than from too little. Let the fingertip test be your guide.

Using Your Herbs

The joy of having fresh herbs is using them. To help you do that, some great recipes are included in this section. The Herbed Roast Pork (right) is easy and gets raves. The Herbed Pasta (page 108) is probably the easiest pasta dish ever created. Each of these dishes can stand alone but serve them Italian style — the pasta first, then the roast, and then the salad. Finish it off with fresh fruit and cheese, a cup of espresso and some Sambuca, and you have a feast!

Recipe
Insalata Caprese

Fresh ripe red and/or yellow tomatoes (1 per person)

Fresh mozzarella cheese

Extra virgin olive oil

Garlic cloves, minced

Balsamic vinegar

Salt

Basil leaves, shredded

Pepper

Fresh Italian bread

1 Cut tomatoes and mozzarella cheese into slices. Arrange slices on serving plate, alternating tomatoes with cheese. (The salad is more eye-appealing if red and yellow tomatoes are arranged to alternate with the cheese.) Sprinkle with basil, garlic, salt and pepper. Drizzle with olive oil; dot with vinegar. (Use about 5 parts oil to 1 part vinegar.) After eating salad, mop up garlic vinaigrette with Italian bread. My Italian son-in-law, Favio Valentino, gave me this recipe and when I asked if the pasta is topped with Romano or Parmesan cheese, he answered most emphatically, "Absolutely not. Never!"

The Insalata can be served as a first main course on individual plates, as a main dish entree on a big platter, or as a salad following the pasta or meat entree.

Recipe
Herbed Roasted Pork

1 boneless pork loin (6 to 10 inches long)

5 (6-inch) sprigs rosemary

10 to 20 sage leaves

3 to 4 garlic cloves

1 tablespoon salt

½ teaspoon pepper

1 to 2 tablespoons olive oil

1 cup chicken broth

1 cup white wine

2 to 3 tablespoons flour

10 oz. sliced fresh mushrooms

1 Heat oven to 400°F Score fat side of pork loin by cutting crisscross slashes about 1 inch apart through fat but not into meat. Strip leaves from rosemary sprigs.

2 On cutting board, combine rosemary leaves, sage leaves and garlic. Chop until finely minced. In small bowl, combine minced herbs and garlic, salt, pepper and enough olive oil to make a paste. Rub herb mixture over pork, working it into crisscross slashes.

3 Place pork in shallow roasting pan. Bake for 20 minutes. Reduce oven temperature to 325°F; add one-half cup chicken broth to pan. Bake an additional 40 to 45 minutes, adding chicken broth (or water) to keep liquid in pan during baking. Remove pork from pan; place on serving platter. Let rest 15 minutes.

4 Meanwhile, place roasting pan over medium heat. Add wine and remaining chicken broth to pan; scrape bottom of pan to loosen any brown bits from pork. Gradually whisk in flour, cooking and stirring until sauce boils and thickens. Add half of the mushrooms; cook until sauce is reduced to one-third its volume. (Mushrooms will shrink during cooking.)

5 Just before serving, add remaining mushrooms to sauce; cook just until thoroughly heated. Cut pork into ½- to 1-inch-thick slices; place on serving platter. Pour sauce over pork. If desired, serve with hot cooked rice, or mashed or roasted potatoes.

Spring in a Bowl

Forcing bulbs and branches adds a burst of color to winter's dark days.

Even in the dead of winter you can have a bright floral display.

Bringing spring indoors a bit early is a tradition for many gardeners. One good way to shake the winter doldrums is by forcing flowers to bloom indoors. The resulting show brightens any mood, lifts our spirits and reminds us that Mother Nature is preparing her spring wardrobe for us to enjoy. Plus, forcing is easy and rewarding. After all, florists rely on this method for an abundance of fragrance, flowers and color, so there is no reason why you shouldn't share in the fun and rewards.

"Forcing" refers to a process that stimulates flowers and bulbs to bloom out of their normal season. Although the word implies harshness, the exercise is really a rather gentle one — more of a coaxing or persuading. Forcing, in simple terms, tricks a flower into opening before it would have on its own.

A wide variety of plants can be forced. The most familiar may be the spring-blooming bulbs, which can be persuaded that they have already slept through winter to bloom on your schedule. Then there are those two winter standouts, paperwhite narcissus and amaryllis, both bulbs that bloom reliably in winter without any special treatment. Third, after the cold weather has set in for real outside, it's time to start thinking of forcing branches of spring-blooming shrubs and trees.

The following pages offer some simple tricks that will help you enjoy your own abundance of bloom during the dreary days of winter.

Getting Started

First, let's talk about spring-blooming bulbs, one of the most commonly forced plants in winter.

The easiest spring bulbs to force are muscaris (grape hyacinths) and hyacinths, although many others will work, as well. Tulips, crocuses and daffodils are also good choices. Many of these bulbs can be purchased right now at your local nursery.

Whichever bulbs you pick, choose early varieties that are among the first to bloom naturally in a garden.

Emerging hyacinths.

After selecting your bulbs, you will need a container with good drainage. If you plan to use new terra-cotta pots in which to plant your bulbs, soak the pots in water for a few hours before planting so they won't absorb water away from the plant roots.

For the spring bloomers mentioned above, choose a soil-free potting medium that will hold moisture while allowing the bulb roots to develop. To plant, use as many bulbs as will fit in the pot you've selected. Plant bulbs pointed end up so that just the top of the bulb is visible above the soil line, about an inch below the rim of the pot. Now water them thoroughly — a crucial step.

Chilling Your Bulbs

Once you have planted your bulbs, it's time to give them the cold shoulder: Most spring-blooming bulbs need a period of cold to trigger the process that initiates blooming. In nature this cold treatment hap-

Cluster forced bulbs and branches in front of a window for a preview of spring.

Hyacinths are a classic for the "bulb jar."

happens in a garden over four or five months, during which time the bulbs' roots and stems develop and the flower buds get ready to open.

One pan of fragrant hyacinths can perfume a large room.

To simulate this process indoors, bulbs need 12 to 14 weeks of cold storage at 40°F to 50°F. This "cold treatment" allows roots to develop and blooms to form. If you live in a climate that provides the requisite temperature, you can pot up your bulbs and leave them outdoors. For gardeners in areas where winter temperatures aren't so reliable, store your bulbs in a very cool basement, garage, shed or refrigerator as a substitute for the natural cold. If you use a refrigerator, be sure to remove all fruits and vegetables stored in it. As fruits ripen, they release ethylene gas, a natural product that damages bulbs.

Some companies do sell pre-chilled bulbs that are intended to provide fall bloom. However, once bulbs are removed from the cold treatment, bulbs must be planted soon afterward or the effect of the cold treatment quickly vanishes.

Hyacinth bulbs are one commonly available example of these pre-chilled bulbs. Ready-to-force hyacinths can be purchased in kits along with a special vase. The vase has a pinched and flared neck that supports the bulb and keeps it suspended just above the water level. These pre-cooled hyacinths will bloom about two weeks earlier than ones that aren't pre-cooled.

To force these hyacinths, put the bulb in the vase, add water to just below the bulb, and place the container in a spot with moderate light and temperature. You'll be able to watch the roots form and develop as the hyacinth grows and produces incredibly fragrant blossoms.

Potted bulbs must be kept moist but not wet during this period of cold treatment; check frequently to see that the bulbs don't dry out. An open plastic bag placed loosely over each pot will help with moisture retention.

When the required cold period is over, move the pots to a spot that provides warmer temperatures (around 55°F) and indirect light for a couple of weeks. Then move the pots to a sunny, cool area and you should see blooms in another two to four weeks.

Tulips need a period of cold before they will flower.

Mix bulbs together for variety.

One important note: Gardeners often wonder what to do with forced bulbs after they have bloomed. Put simply, throw them away. Unfortunately, with the exception of amaryllis (see the sidebar on page 115), the forcing process takes a lot of energy from bulbs and most never bloom the same again. Toss your forced bulbs in the compost pile once their show is over and plan to buy new bulbs for other uses.

Making Your Choice

While spring-blooming bulbs are a common choice for forcing, they are not the only reliable winter performers. Amaryllis and paperwhite narcissus bulbs are two favorites that do not require pre-cooling and will give even the first-time forcer great results.

Paperwhites are great for forcing, probably because they are so easy to grow. They can be purchased in early fall as loose bulbs from garden centers and mail-order suppliers, and in six or seven weeks they can be brought into bloom.

Paperwhites are best forced by planting them in gravel or a similar medium. (You can sometimes substitute marbles, colored stones

Hyacinth bulbs may irritate sensitive skin; wear gloves when handling them.

New hyacinth buds are ghostly pale.

Paperwhites don't require chilling and are among the easiest bulbs to force.

or beach glass for the gravel for a more decorative look.) In autumn, you can frequently find paperwhites in stores as part of a kit that contains a shallow, no-drainage-hole pot and a supply of gravel.

If you plan to force a number of paperwhites, consider purchasing some special "bulb pans" made of terra-cotta or other materials. These pans are shallow — a bit deeper than a terra-cotta saucer — and are usually waterproof with no drainage hole.

Fill your container two-thirds full with the non-soil medium of your choice. Place as many bulbs as you can fit directly on the medium with the pointed end up — the more bulbs, the better. Then fill in around the bulbs with medium, leaving the top of the bulbs exposed. Add water until it barely reaches the base of the bulbs and set them in a cool (45°F to 50°F), dark place. Check the water level frequently and throughout the process. Keep the water level just below the bulbs' bases. In about three weeks, roots should have formed and you should see green shoots

coming out of the tops of the bulbs.

At this stage, move the paperwhites to a cool and sunny spot. In about three or four weeks you should have masses of sweetly scented white flowers on display.

Amazing Amaryllis

Amaryllis bulbs are another favorite. Their flowers are large and striking — a perfect accent point for holiday entertaining. Colors range from pristine white to deep, vibrant red, and some multicolors, such as 'Apple Blossom', are unusual and showy.

Like paperwhites, amaryllis bulbs do not need to be pre-chilled, and they are often available in fall in a pre-packaged kit. Because of their larger size, they normally are planted one to a pot.

If you use a pre-packaged kit, follow the directions provided. Otherwise, choose a pot that is just a bit larger than the amaryllis bulb. The pot should have good drainage. Fill the pot with a few inches of potting soil, place the bulb in the pot with the pointed end facing up, and fill in around the bulb with more soil. The top 2 or 3 inches of the bulb should be above the soil line. Water well, even letting the water run through the pot a couple of times to be sure that the soil is fully saturated, and put the pot in a cool yet sunny spot. Water as needed until the first

Amaryllis sports extraordinary blooms.

green shoots appear from the top of the bulb, which should happen in two or three weeks.

Once the green shoots appear, water more often and in four to six weeks, you should have several huge, magnificent, velvety flowers.

Garden Tip
Re-Blooming an Amaryllis

After forcing an amaryllis to bloom indoors, you can save the bulb for next year. To do this, cut off the flower stem a few inches above the bulb after the flowers are spent. Don't remove the leaves. Let the plant continue to grow in a warm and bright location. Water regularly and fertilize once a month with a water-soluble house plant fertilizer. You can move the plant outside once warm weather returns. Place it in a partly sunny location. Before the first frost, bring it indoors. Stop watering and fertilizing around September 1 or so. Let the amaryllis "rest" in a cool location for three months. On December 1, unpot the bulb and clean off any dead material, being careful not to damage the roots. (The roots should be healthy and firm.) Repot the amaryllis bulb in fresh potting soil and repeat the steps for forcing amaryllis found on page 114.

About two months after you resume watering, you should see the dramatic blooms open.

Special occasion? Plan ahead and you can force bulbs for a lavish display.

Branching Out

Another way to bring color into your home in winter is to force branches of flowering shrubs and trees that normally bloom in the spring. Forsythia, pussy willow, witch hazel, flowering quince, spiraea and most fruit trees are perfect candidates for forcing.

To force branches successfully, you'll need to gather them at the optimum time. Buds that are completely dormant won't open, so wait to cut your branches until you see swollen buds. Depending on your location, this may happen by mid- to late winter when temperatures are above freezing. Branches cut at this time should burst into bloom with just a bit of coaxing.

Cut branches from your selected plant and bring them indoors. (Be sure that your cuts are sharp and clean.) The branches will need to be given a bath so their cells can absorb the moisture needed to open the flowers. Commandeer the bathtub for this process and fill it with enough slightly warm water to just cover the branches. I leave the branches to soak in the tub all day, and then stand them upright in buckets of water amended with a packet of floral preservative.

An old recommendation says to cut or crush the bottom of the stem of the branches at this point. However, if you don't, the branches seem to still bloom just fine. A large plastic bag placed over both branches and bucket helps hold in humidity, however.

Change the water every day or so, and within a few days, the buds should show color.

Once color is evident, remove the plastic bag and arrange the branches in a vase. They should bloom shortly.

Early-blooming magnolias are especially elegant.

Forced branches of forsythia, pear blossoms and flowering quince

Serviceberries and flowering quince are natural partners.

Garden Tip
Buy Your Branches

One innovative gardener obtains branches for forcing in a rather novel way: At the end of her gardening season in late fall, she has found that many garden centers have great sales on container-grown flowering trees and shrubs.

She purchases the container-grown bloomers she wants at sale prices and then puts them in a protected place in her yard. She either sinks the pots into the ground or covers them with mulch and burlap for insulation to keep the roots from freezing. Then, when the buds begin to swell in early spring, she cuts all the branches off and follows the procedure for forcing them into bloom. She discards what is left of the plants because she never intended to grow them in the first place. Instead, she sacrifices them in order to fill her home with life and color before Mother Nature can even think about filling her garden with the same thing.

Yellow forsythia.

Pink quince.

Spring-flowering bulbs and branches make precious little packages of color and fragrance. With a minimum investment of time and effort, you can persuade them to share their gifts on your time-table instead of Mother Nature's.

Once buds have swelled on spring-blooming shrubs, you can force branches.

White flowering quince blossoms.

PICTURE-PERFECT HOUSEPLANTS

Although they provide pleasure year-round, house plants are vitally important in winter, when you want something fresh and green in your home.

It is one of the great paradoxes of life: Those natural green thumbs who effortlessly grow prize-winning dahlias and gigantic tomatoes outdoors frequently turn into grim reapers when it comes to houseplants. Frustrated, these gardeners eventually start to treat houseplants as cut flowers — simply throwing out any plants that die and buying more.

On the other side of the spectrum are houseplant wizards. These gardeners have homes that resemble jungles filled with hibiscus plants, monster-sized rubber trees, and bananas. These indoor green thumbs have learned the formula for houseplant success — proper light levels, adequate humidity and the right plant in the right place.

If you'd like to improve your indoor garden this winter, here are a few tips for keeping your houseplants healthy. We've also included descriptions of several great plants that thrive indoors (including a few nearly indestructible plants that will grow even under the most challenging conditions).

Getting The Light Right

All the good intentions in the world won't let you grow fabulous houseplants unless you provide your plants with the proper amount of light. Each plant needs a certain amount of light to thrive, and if you can't meet that requirement, kiss the plant goodbye. It may hang on for a month or two, looking pale and dropping its leaves, but ultimately it will die.

Houseplants usually come with a tag that lists their light requirements — low, medium or bright. To establish what kind of light you have in your home, look at how much sunlight streams through the windows. The most intense light comes from

Norfolk Island pines are tidy houseplants with an architectural look.

Monstera leaves are bold.

Parlor palms will tolerate low light.

south windows. Next in intensity are east- and west-facing windows. North windows let in the least amount of sunlight. Other factors influence window light, too. Overhangs, leafed-out deciduous or ever-green trees, window coverings, the color of interior walls and floor coverings, dust and UV coatings on windows, and the time of year all diminish or increase the sunlight available to your house-plants.

The human eye is not a good judge of light. It adjusts to light levels rather than distinguish-ing between them. One way to determine how much interior light is available in a location is to use a camera with a built-in light meter. If you don't own such a camera, ask a friend who does to help.

Set the camera's film speed to ASA100. Lay a piece of white paper in the spot where you plan to place your plant, and aim the camera at the paper.

Be sure not to block light from the paper or cast a shadow with the camera. Set the camera to an f4 stop. Then look at the shutter speed reading. This reading will give the approximate light intensity in

The easy-care philodendron.

While some citrus may fruit indoors, most require more light to set fruit than is found in the average home.

A scented geranium trained as a standard

"foot-candles," a standard measure of light intensity. For example, a reading of 1/60 shutter speed translates to 60 foot-candles. Low light, as measured by a camera light meter, is anything below 400 foot-candles or 1/400 shutter speed. Medium light ranges from 400 to 1,000 foot-candles, or 1/1,000 shutter speed. Anything reading above 1/1,000 is bright light.

If you don't have a camera available, here is another guideline to help you identify how much light a location receives.

Variegated houseplants, such as this hoya or wax plant, need more light than their all-green cousins.

- **Low light:** You'll find low light within 2 feet of a north-facing window; 8 to 10 feet from an east or west window, or 12 inches from one 40-watt fluorescent light.

- **Medium light:** You'll find medium light within 2 feet of an east window or west window; 2 to 4 feet from a south window that is curtained, or 12 inches from two 40-watt fluorescent lights.

- **Bright light:** You'll find bright light within 2 feet of a large southeast-, south- or southwest-facing window, or within 2 feet of an east or west window that also has four 40-watt fluorescent lights within 12 inches of plant tops.

Birds' nest ferns love humidity.

Flowering maples add a splash of color.

Adjusting The Brightness

White walls and light carpeting will reflect light back onto plants, helping to brighten the exposure, just as dark wood paneling and brown carpets reduce the available light. You can remedy dim surroundings by painting the surfaces around houseplants with white paint, or covering the surfaces with aluminum foil to reflect light onto plants.

If your windows and rooms are less than bright, don't despair. Supplemental lights can turn any location, even ones without windows, into an acceptable area for most plants.

Fluorescent lights can either augment or replace natural light. Sunlight has blue and red tones that stimulate plant growth. A regular fluorescent light tube that is marked "cool white" contains mostly blue tones. Use it as one of the lights in a double fixture.

The other should be a tube that contains red tones. Aquarium lights are red and so are tubes marked "warm white" lights. Look in the light bulb section of your local discount center to find these fluorescent tubes. (Typical incandescent bulbs produce more heat than fluorescent bulbs. To provide enough light intensity for plant growth, incandescent bulbs would need to be placed so close to plants that their heat would likely damage plants.)

Fluorescent lights should be 12 inches from plant tops to provide maximum intensity. Hang the fixture from the ceiling by chain or rope. That way, as plants grow taller, you can raise the fixture. Lights should be on at least 14 hours a day to simulate summer sunlight. Timers are the easiest way to turn lights off and on, especially if you are not home. Set the timer to turn on at

Set African violets on pebble trays to boost humidity.

7 a.m. and off at 10 p.m.

And, remember that plants grow toward a light source, so they should be turned every week or two to keep them growing straight.

Try These

Houseplants for Low-Light Areas

Are you hoping to brighten up a room that receives little light? Try one of these low-light performers.

Philodendron scandens (heart-leafed philodendron)
This is a vine with dark green, heart-shaped leaves. Clip ends off growing shoots to keep the vines compact. Fertilize once a month; allow soil to dry out between waterings.

Schefflera spp. (octopus tree)
Scheffleras are trees with dark green leaves. The plants tolerate low-light conditions; they grow larger and faster in brighter spots. Allow the soil surface to dry between waterings; fertilize monthly.

Chlorophytum commosum (airplane or spider plant)
Spider plants just seem to grow and grow, no matter what the conditions are. Plus, they make a lot of little plants (which are great gifts to other gardeners). Place the plants in a spot with low to medium light and water when the soil surface dries.

Aspidistra elatior (cast-iron plant)
These old-fashioned plants have dark green leaves and tolerate low light. Cast-iron plants can reach 2 feet tall. The plants require little humidity and fertilizer; water them when the top couple of inches of the soil have dried.

Sansevieria trifasciata (mother-in-law's tongue or snakeplant)
So named for its sharp, sword-like leaves, the snake-plant thrives in just about any condition from low to bright light. Be sure to allow the soil surface to dry between waterings. Snakeplants can tolerate low humidity.

Providing Enough Humidity

Although light is a crucial factor in healthy houseplant growth, the second most important element — humidity — can be easier to forget. Dry air will brown a moisture-lover such as a fern as fast as clammy air will cause rot and death for an aloe. During winter, artificial heating creates drier air, which affects both humans and houseplants.

Humidity levels must match your plants' requirements in order for them to thrive. To raise moisture levels in the air surrounding your plants, set them on trays filled with small pebbles or aquarium gravel and add water to nearly cover the stones. (Be sure pots sit higher than the water level so soil doesn't get waterlogged.) Capillary matting (available at garden centers) is an even simpler way to increase humidity and supply moisture to plants. Line a tray with mats, wet them, and set plant containers on the mats. As the water evaporates, it humidifies the air.

For large numbers of plants that require high humidity, try a portable humidifier.

Bathrooms and kitchens are more humid that the rest of the house. Here, plants such as ferns and bromeliads usually get enough humidity without trays or mats. Ferns, in particular, are naturals for bathrooms, which often are low-light spots due to small or frosted windows. Warm, dry, south-facing rooms are excellent for succulent and citrus plants that thrive in low humidity and bright sun.

Everyday Care

Read and learn — that's the best way to approach caring for a houseplant. For every plant you grow, you should know how often to water and fertilize it, what soil type it prefers and the temperature range in which the plant grows.

In general terms, most houseplants are easy to maintain. They prefer the same temperatures as you do, meaning they do well in most homes. Commercial potting mixes produce healthy plants. These soil-less mixes drain easily, yet retain enough moisture for roots. Also, look for specialty potting mixes for African violets, cacti and other succulents. Use room-temperature water when watering any plant to eliminate stress. Give houseplants a good cleaning periodically. Wipe off leaves every couple of weeks. Household dust can clog stomata — the pores which exchange water vapor and carbon dioxide as the plant "breathes." Books, magazines and the plant-care sheets you can pick up at your local nursery should contain more detailed information. The Internet is another good source for care information. Simply choose your favorite search engine and type in the plant name or type in "houseplants."

That said, some all-time favorites follow on pages 124-125.

Garden Tip
Indoor Problems

Watch for pests such as fungus gnats, mealybugs, spider mitesand aphids. To deter gnats, mulch the soil in containers with a half-inch of sand to keep the surface dry. Yellow "sticky" cards can be placed horizontally near plants to trap some pests. Mealybugs and aphids can sometimes be washed off plants with a strong, lukewarm stream of water. Why not give your plants a shower?

Kill mealybugs with a dab of rubbing alcohol.

Brown leaf tips occur when there is too little humidity.

Spider mites dislike high humidity. Use pebble trays.

Overwatering encourages rot. Water only when necessary.

Mildew loves stressed plants — especially those kept too wet.

Abutilon spp. (flowering maple)

Flowers profusely indoors. Requires bright light and moderate humidity. Will tolerate medium light, but will not flower as freely. Feed every two weeks with a 15-30-15 water-soluble fertilizer, and scratch a tablespoon of lime into the soil every six months.

Araucaria heterophylla (Norfolk Island pine)

Makes an architectural statement in rooms. Does best in medium light with moderate humidity. Can tolerate periods of low light or direct sunlight in the winter months. Water sparingly; feed every few months in winter. When new growth appears, feed every two weeks; water when soil surface dries. Be

Rubber plants are tough and can survive lower light and drier conditions.

sure the water does not contain lots of lime; avoid water softened mechanically, too.

Asplenium nidus (bird's nest fern)

Tidy and attractive year-round. This fern has no messy, brown fronds that drop continually. Requires low to medium light and moderate humidity — bathrooms are perfect. Otherwise, group with other plants for added humidity. Feed every two weeks with a high-nitrogen plant food.

Chamaedorea elegans (parlor palm)

Tolerant of low light. Place near an east or west window; likes low to moderate humidity. Fertilize monthly in winter; water sparingly. When new growth begins, feed every two weeks and water when soil surface is dry. Fast growing; can reach 6 feet indoors.

Citrus limon (lemon)

Should fruit indoors. Blossoms appear in midwinter through late spring and perfume the house with their sweet scent. To pollinate, take a paintbrush and dust each flower (passing from flower to flower). Requires bright light and low humidity. Water when soil surface is dry. Feed every time you water with fertilizer formulated for acid-loving plants or one for citrus.

Ficus elastica (rubber tree)

Nearly indestructible. Rubber trees have thick leaves that are dark green or flushed with purple. The plants tolerate low light, but do much better in medium or bright light. Water only when the top couple of inches of potting mix become dry. Feed with a foliage plant food monthly.

Hoya carnosa (wax plant)

Ideal for hanging baskets. Tolerates low light, but prefers medium; needs little humidity. Waxy, compound pink flowers appear in summer, especially if the plant is grown outdoors under a tree for the warm months. Fertilize three times a year — early spring, again in June and late August. Water sparingly.

Monstera deliciosa (Swiss cheese plant)

Best if trained up a moss-filled pole. Thrives in low light and medium humidity. Do not put in full sun; leaves will burn and the plant will decline rapidly. Fertilize once in late autumn and again in midwinter. When growth resumes in spring, fertilize every two weeks. Water when soil surface is dry. If grown in moderate light, plant may flower and produce a fruit. Put outdoors in full shade during summer to accelerate flowering.

Pelargonium 'Graveolens' (rose geranium)

Leaves have the heady aroma of lemon and roses. Tiny, pale pink flowers appear in spring. Lacy leaves are used to flavor sugar, syrups, cakes and fruit salads, and to make perfume. Place in medium to bright light and don't worry about humidity. Water when soil surface is dry. Feed every two weeks with 15-30-15 fertilizer.

Phalaenopsis hybrids (moth orchid)

Easy to grow. Will flower most of the year in medium light. A windowsill with morning sun is perfect. Requires high humidity — pebble tray or capillary mat is necessary. Water when growing medium (usually shredded bark and/or peat) is dry. Feed with diluted orchid fertilizer every time you water. Flower stalks appear in autumn when nighttime temperatures drop. Blooms start in winter. Cut the stalk back to last fading flower, and another set of blooms will be produced.

Rosmarinus officinalis (rosemary)

Belongs on every kitchen windowsill for its fragrance. Requires medium to bright light and good humidity. Water sparingly. Feed every six weeks. Add 2 to 3 tablespoons of lime to soil when planting and scratch into soil another tablespoon of lime in spring to maintain the sweet soil rosemary loves.

Rosemary is sometimes troubled by spider mites indoors. But it is a resilient plant.

Saintpaulia hybrids (African violet)

Blooms year-round. Needs medium to bright light; no direct sun. Self-watering pots or a capillary mat will supply the humidity needed. Water when soil surface is dry. Use room-temperature water; take care not to wet leaves or plant crown. Or, soak pots in a few inches of water for 20 minutes. Feed every two weeks with a flowering plant fertilizer. Reduce feeding to monthly when plants stop flowering.

Moth orchids flower extravagantly indoors.

THE GARDEN IN WINTER

Enjoy your garden every season of the year. Just add plants and structures that provide winter interest. Here are the secrets.

Frosty plumes of Miscanthus sinensis 'Silver Feather' sparkle against a winter sky.

As you look up from your seed catalog in the middle of winter, what do you see outside your window? Do you see grasses rising gracefully out of the snow and blue-tinged conifers outlined in white? Do you gaze at wintergreen laden with berries, and birches showing off their papery bark? Or do you look at a lifeless plot of land, bury your head and wait for spring? If you're in the latter category, you're missing a whole season of splendor — a season that doesn't require a lot of upkeep, just some initial planning and planting. To get started, keep in mind the following suggestions. You may even warm up to the whole idea of winter.

Frame the Garden

Since shape is essential to the winter garden, choose large items to anchor your space and offer a variety of forms and colors. Tall evergreens will give you the green you crave and help your garden in numerous ways. You can plant a row of conifers such as Leyland cypress (*x Cupressocyparis leylandii*, Zones 6 to 9) to provide a privacy wall, form a backdrop for smaller plants, create a noise barrier or lend a formal look to your landscape.

Evergreen trees are also stately focal points with much-needed color during dreary weather. Red cedar (*Juniperus virginiana*, Zones 3 to 9), for instance, boasts reddish brown bark, dark blue fruit and gray-green needles with yellow tips.

Evergreen hedges complement a winter garden. Whether you're looking to border an outdoor room, create a natural fence or divide areas of your yard, hedges help tidy up an area and look stunning topped with snow. One of the hardiest for northern gardens is wintergreen (*Gaultheria procumbens*, Zones 3 to 8), though some areas can use shrubs like boxwood (*Buxus microphylla*, Zones 6 to 9) and cotoneaster (*Cotoneaster lucidus*, Zones 3 to 7) for hedging, as well. And tightly clipped hedges, cut very short, can be used to border a flower bed or herb garden, or to line a pathway.

Remember the importance of deciduous trees — their many advantages are critical to your plan. Some species sport beautiful bark, like the amur cherry (*Prunus maackii*, Zones 3 to 7) with its coppery-colored peeling trunk.

Others, like Washington hawthorn (*Crataegus phaenopyrum*, Zones 4 to 8), hold their brightly colored fruit all winter long. Some trees are gorgeous simply for their shape. Look for specimens with horizontal branching like the crabapple (*Malus 'Adirondack'*, Zones 5 to 8), or unusual shapes like the European weeping ash (*Fraxinus excelsior 'Pendula'*, Zones 5 to 8), whose drooping branches resemble an umbrella.

Framing also comes in the form of manmade structures. An arbor laced with clematis (*Clematis 'Jackmanii'*, Zones 4 to 9) or honeysuckle (*Lonicera 'Dropmore Scarlet'*, Zones 4 to 9) forms a stunning

Evergreen hedges bring structure to a winter garden.

archway when covered with snow. A pergola sheltering a bench becomes a sitting area you'll enjoy all winter. Even an old shed can be attractive if it displays a window box lined with evergreens.

Natural structures bring a sense of age and place to a garden; with them, a space feels more peaceful and calm. An old limestone wall, a waterfall that works year-round, a grouping of artistically placed boulders — all these will bring dimension to your developing space.

Add Detail

If, in the past, you have chosen shrubs for their attractive characteristics in spring, summer or autumn, this year add winter interest and wildlife attraction to your criteria. Plants that offer shelter, colorful stems, and fruit throughout the cold season will please not only you but the birds, as well. A red osier dogwood (*Cornus stolonifera*, Zones 2 to 8), with its bright-red winter stems, for example, will lure birds to its branches daily.

Other plants provide winter blooms and delicate scents — rare treats this time of year. Most, like witch hazel (*Hamamelis mollis*, Zones 5 to 9), with spidery yellow to red flowers and a sweet scent, are hardy to Zone 5. If you live farther north, try winter aconite (*Eranthis hyemalis*, Zones

4 to 9) and talk to a local nursery grower for other suggestions — some less hardy plants may still survive in your plot if they're well protected.

Perennials with appealing seedpods and flower heads will beckon cardinals and blue jays year-round and bring texture to your space. Black-eyed Susan (*Rudbeckia fulgida*, Zones 4 to 9), purple coneflower (*Echinacea purpurea*, Zones 3 to 9), blue wild indigo (*Baptisia australis*, Zones 3 to 9), and butterfly weed (*Asclepias tuberosa*, Zones 4 to 9) are good choices. Dried blossoms, whether they're the big blooms of hydrangeas (*Hydrangea paniculata*, Zones 4 to 8) or the flat heads

Ornamental grasses and perennials provide winter interest in a border.

Garlic chives offer seed heads that catch snow.

Witch hazel bears spidery flowers in winter.

of yarrows (*Achillea* spp., Zones 3 to 9) are also eye-catching when dusted with snow or encased in ice.

Some of the most dramatic plants in winter are ornamental grasses. The straw-colored plumes of silver grass (*Miscanthus sinensis*, Zones 4 to 9) or Japanese blood grass (*Imperata cylindrica* 'Red Baron', Zones 4 to 9) give a soft, natural look to a hard, cold landscape. Plant grasses in front of a group of evergreens or another spot where their light plumes will shine against a dark background.

American holly is a large evergreen shrub or small tree with crimson fruit that stays.

Iris reticulata *flowers in late winter or early spring.*

Provide Accents

Finally, if you want to add more personality and interest to your winter garden, add small accents. Against a snowy backdrop, dark statues or urns made of lead or bronze draw attention more than those of marble or limestone. Choose an object with a horizontal feature that will create icicles on melting days. Unique birdhouses, birdbaths, reflecting spheres or brightly painted folk art provide visual relief when your flowers fade away. And simple pots filled with branches of bittersweet (*Celastrus scandens*, Zones 3 to 8) add texture to a deck or porch. There are thousands of ways to show your style in a winter garden — all you need is to think of winter in a whole new way.

Manmade elements provide personality and contrast.

Variety — a mix of hardwoods, softwoods, grasses and manmade elements — makes for an attractive garden in winter.

Try These
More Plants for Winter Interest

American cranberry bush (*Viburnum trilobum*, Zones 2 to 7): Shrub with red fruits that persist into winter.

Arrowwood (*Viburnum dentatum*, Zones 3 to 8): Shrub with blue-black fruits that persist into winter.

Beautyberry (*Callicarpa americana*, Zones 5 to 9): Shrub with purple berries that persist in winter.

Bloodtwig dogwood (*Cornus sanguinea*, Zones 5 to 7): Shrub with reddish-green winter stems.

Christmas rose (*Helleborus niger*, Zones 4 to 8): Perennial with pinkish-white flowers from early winter to spring.

Corkscrew hazel (*Corylus avellana 'Contorta'*): Shrub with twisted, curly branches.

Crape myrtle (*Lagerstroemia indica*, Zones 7 to 9): Trees with peeling bark.

Cyclamen (*Cyclamen coum*, Zones 5 to 9): Perennial with white or pink flowers in winter or early spring.

Dragon-claw willow (*Salix 'Tortuosa'*, Zones 6 to 9): Tree with weeping twisted curly branches.

English holly (*Ilex aquifolium*, Zones 7 to 9): Tree with red or yellow fruits that persist into winter.

Flame willow (*Salix 'Britzensis'*, Zones 4 to 9): Shrub with branches that turn bright orange-red in winter.

Grape holly (*Mahonia japonica*, Zones 7 to 8): Shrub with fragrant yellow flowers in winter.

Hawthorn (*Crataegus viridis 'Winter King'*, Zones 5 to 7): Tree with red fruits that persist through winter.

Lacebark pine (*Pinus bungeana*, Zones 6 to 8): Evergreen tree with bark that peels to reveal contrasting color.

Moosewood maple (*Acer pensylvanicum*, Zones 3 to 7): Tree with green-and-white-striped bark.

Ninebark (*Physocarpus opulifolius*, Zones 3 to 7): Shrub with attractive peeling bark.

Pagoda dogwood (*Cornus alternifolia*, Zones 4 to 8): Shrub or tree with a very horizontal branching pattern.

Paper birch (*Betula papyrifera*, Zones 2 to 7): Tree with peeling ivory-white bark.

Paperbark maple (*Acer griseum*, Zones 4 to 8): Small tree with peeling bark.

Red osier dogwood (*Cornus stolonifera*, Zones 2 to 8): Shrub with bright-red or yellow winter stems.

Red-twig dogwood (*Cornus alba*, Zones 2 to 8): Shrub with bright-red winter stems

River birch (*Betula nigra 'Heritage'*, Zones 4 to 9): Tree with attractive, peeling bark.

Washington hawthorn (*Crataegus phaenopyrum*, Zones 4 to 8): Thorny tree with red fruits that persist through winter.

White forsythia (*Abeliophyllum distichum*, Zones 5 to 9): Shrub with fragrant white flowers in late winter and early spring.

Winter daphne (*Daphne odora*, Zones 7 to 9): Shrub with fragrant pink or white flowers in midwinter or early spring.

Winter heath (*Erica carnea*, Zones 5 to 7): Shrub with pink, purple, or white flowers in late winter and early spring.

Winter jasmine (*Jasminum nudiflorum*, Zones 6 to 9): Shrub with yellow flowers in winter and early spring.

Winterberry (*Ilex verticillata*, Zones 5 to 8): Shrub with red or yellow fruits that persist into winter.

DRAFT A LANDSCAPE

Winter is the perfect time to take stock of your yard ... and plan for next season.

When the temperature drops below freezing, and the snow starts flying, don't feel sorry for your gardening self. Instead, get busy and start making plans for next spring. Drafting a good landscape plan may well be your most important gardening activity!

Get out graph paper, a 100-foot measuring tape, and a stack of mailorder catalogs. Spend winter months plotting, planning and ordering plants. The time spent drafting a garden plan and thinking through strategies can be the smartest thing you can do. You'll save yourself endless mistakes. And with the advance planning, your new garden can be a traffic-stopper in its first year.

Garden plans are not only for entire yards. They can also solve thorny small problems such as what to plant in the narrow, shady, bone-dry strip next to the garage. When planned in advance, even vegetable gardens are simpler to plant and more productive because you make maximum use of your space. Yard makeovers, too, are easier when planned on paper. Sketch in what you want to save and plan around it.

Use time available in winter to make detailed plans for the upcoming gardening year.

Winter planning means summer success.

Winter gives you time to really plan out what will look great.

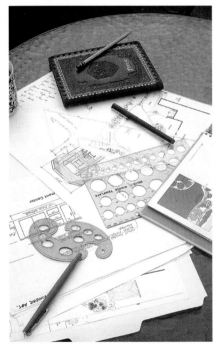

Whether you use pen and paper or a computer-driven drafting program, the slower months of fall and winter are an excellent time to plan additions to your landscape. You'll also have plenty of time to order new plants.

Making a map

The first step to any garden plan is to measure everything in your yard — and that means everything — even if you are only contemplating a new perennial border along a fence. The reason for such thoroughness is that your border can be affected by a tree or building 30 or even 50 feet away — the tree's shadow will limit your plant selections. Whether you use graph paper and a pencil or computer software to create a master plan, these measurements have to be made the old-fashioned way — with a tape measure and a trusty sidekick to hold one end. Those tools are the basis of any well-laid plan.

In one case, the landscape offered four towering trees in the back yard and no vegetation other than grass. Two 60-foot maples and two 40-foot Colorado blue spruces combined to create a shady yard, even though it faces south. This gardener had to map everything with meticulous care to find sunny areas in which to plant.

Goals and observations

Next, determine what the end result of your garden plan will be. Is a water garden your goal? Do you want to integrate vegetable beds into an existing landscape? Do you need to add attractive shrubs and trees to accent your walkways? Or are floral borders with four-season appeal your objective? Visualize the finished project and make a list of its components. Include plants desired, soil amendments, border or paving materials, and decorative objects like arbors, birdbaths, and sundials.

Maybe your goals include an edible landscape border along the back fence, a rose garden, a kitchen garden, and wide curving perennial beds to flank the house.

Make a list of materials and plants and then consider where to

Making the plan.

Mass color for the biggest impact.

place them. On your graph paper plan, you may have drawn the trees, but have no idea how far their shadows spread. So watch the sun. Look at where the shadows are in the early morning. Later, note what sections of the yard were in the sun at noon and again at 3 p.m. After six weeks of observation, you'll have a pretty good idea of where the sunny spots were when the trees are fully covered with leaves.

Examine your landscape in detail before you plant. You'll save yourself extra work, disappointment, and expense. One gardener learned this lesson the hard way, spending $150 and days of labor to plant a peach mini-orchard in their Texas yard. The trees died from root rot within months. This disaster could have been avoided by watching where the water tended to pool in the yard after a heavy rain and where the water drained quickly.

Once you have spent time looking at your project area and studied the possible pitfalls, sketch in beds, shrubs, and other features on your plan. Then consider how they will look in proportion to one another, the surrounding yard, and structures like a house, fence, or deck. Remember to use the mature size of a shrub, flower, or tree when plotting. Nothing is worse than having to yank out a 4-foot-wide hydrangea because it has outgrown the 2 feet you allotted it. This is where computer software programs do have an advantage over graph paper. Three-D simulations on the computer screen provide an instant snapshot of the future when plants are mature.

Layers of plants accentuate each other and draw the eye into the garden.

Your best early tool is a tape measure. Measure everything and keep track of moving sun and shade.

All plants need well-amended ground in which to grow. A soil test will reveal any nutrient deficiencies.

"Hardscape," such as paths, patios, and so on, are best planned and finished before you start adding plants.

Whatever look you choose, upgrading your landscape is always an excellent investment in your home.

Picking plants

After deciding where to place beds and gardens, dig into a pile of catalogs from seed and plant companies.

Catalogs are an invaluable information source. Many of them list plants by growing conditions such as shade and wet ground, full sun and dry soil, or shade and dry soil. Most give at least a thumbnail description of required growing conditions and the height and width of mature plants. They also list the USDA climate zones in which a plant will flourish, helping you to determine what is suitable for your area. Local nurseries may have plant lists or catalogs of their stock, too. And your local county extension agency usually has plant lists of varieties that do well in your climate. All these sources are helpful when making selections.

After ordering plants from catalogs (do this in the winter months for best selection and schedule deliveries for after your last freeze), make lists of plants to buy locally and materials needed such as fertilizer, topsoil, or a pool liner, if you want to add a water feature. Keep your eyes open for bargains in the cold-weather months.

Also make a list of decorative objects you want to include in your garden, plan and give the list to your family when they ask what you want for holiday presents.

Scheduling the work

The last step in making a garden plan is to outline a work schedule — progressive steps towards completion. Break up hard labor into manageable pieces that don't tax the body. If you are digging up large amounts of ground, consider renting a rototiller or hiring someone to till.

Work schedules can give you a jump on spring, too. Sunny winter days are perfect for accomplishing the first steps of a garden plan. You can lay out beds and project areas with string and stakes if the ground isn't frozen. You can build borders of rock, brick, and timber, or layer shredded fall leaves over future beds and gardens to mix into the soil later.

When the gardening season finally does arrive, a well-developed plan allows you to quickly complete construction and ground preparations without straining your body. You can have most of your plant material delivered directly to your house, and shop efficiently for the remaining plants and materials from

Dry stream beds are graceful and unique.

a prepared list. Everything will come together easily, and the execution of a much-anticipated entry garden, woodland path, or conifer border will be painless — because you spent the winter making a plan.

Design tricks

Placement and color are everything when you are trying to create a pleasing landscape. Basic design principles and a few tricks from professional landscapers can go a long way to crafting an eye-catching yard.

Start with curved lines. They are more appealing to the eye than long straight borders or edges. The exception is a formal garden, where straight lines define the structure.

Berms (raised planting areas) are a fast, visually effective way to add instant impact to a yard. Use them to block out an offensive view of a parking lot, for instance, and give yourself a colorful vista out the living room window. Flowering shrubs or small trees, surrounded with masses of colorful bed-

Curving pathways please the eye.

A natural focal point can be enhanced with only one or two special plants.

Repeating shapes — like this circle motif — gives a formal feel.

to minimize. Pick just three or four colors and repeat them throughout the yard.

That's all there is to it! Planning your garden in winter makes long evenings inside a little more fun ... and assures gardening success next summer!

ding plants, will turn a berm into an immediate show.

If your garden has a birdbath, sundial, arbor, or bench, make the most of it by planting around it. A circular bed of knee-high flowers such as zinnias, marigolds, and geraniums can turn a plain birdbath into a focal point. Likewise, an asymmetrical patch of flowering thyme, Corsican mint, or chamomile bordered with spiky red salvia will not only draw the eye to a bench but also fill the air with scent. Extend the vertical impact of an arbor with tall, splashy flowers such as hollyhocks and cosmos.

Think color contrast. Red geraniums planted against a red brick house fade into the background; white will stand out. Similarly, you can brighten shady areas with light colors such as white, pale pink, and light blue. Reserve dark tones for white or light backgrounds.

For maximum effect, mass color. Use salmon impatiens and geraniums to border all the flower beds in a yard. Or use one color in the center of a bed and surround it with something with a little contrast. Learn

Accent a path with trees.

COLOR FOR WINTER

Grow African violets indoors. This multi-hued plant family is at its best during the cold winter months.

African violets flower in nearly every color, including yellow.

Native to the tropics and sub-tropics, most of gesneriads (African violets) naturally grow in the shade and are well adapted to the warmth and lower light levels of our homes during the winter.

And best of all, all of these plants flower, either from the leaf axils or terminal spikes. The blossoms come in all shades of the color palette and many are spotted, striped or beautifully blotched with contrasting shades. A few species also have beautifully patterned leaves, worth growing for the foliage alone.

There are minuscule types such as *Sinningia pusilla*, which has tiny lilac blooms and would probably happily live in a thimble if watering were not such a chore. Huge gesneriads such as *Columnea microphylla* may trail as much as 8 feet below their baskets, and are covered with brilliant red flowers in spring. In between are more restrained basket types, rosettes and stemmed species.

Some species of gesneriads have fine fibrous roots, some grow from tubers and some from rhizomes (scaly root sections like tiny spruce

Like African violets, florist's gloxinias come in a range of color and shapes.

cones). The tuberous and rhizomatous types have a dormant period when the plant may appear to die,

Streptocarpus *spp. come from Africa and Asia.*

Gesneriads do well in baskets.

Achimenes *spp. can flower in less than a year from seed.*

Some achimenes grow upright; others trail.

losing its leaves and flowers. Instead, this is a resting period for the plant, after which it will bloom and grow again normally. If you want to time the bloom of your flowers, you can force this dormant period by withholding water. This means you can make plants that ordinarily bloom in summer flower in winter when there is less outdoor color.

Gesneriads require a soil mixture that drains well and most respond to a pH of about 6.5. Grow them in a mix that consists of four parts peat moss, two parts perlite, and one part each of vermiculite and pasteurized soil. Add some crushed eggshells or dolomitic lime for lime-loving species such as resurrection plant (*Achimenes* spp.), flame violet (*Episcia* spp.), and cape primrose (*Streptocarpus* spp.).

Fertilize with 20-20-20 for leafy growth and 15-30-15 for flowers.

You can propagate gesneriads from cuttings (stem section, tip, and leaf), rhizomes, and seeds. Although extremely tiny, the seeds germinate well and grow quickly, often producing flowering plants in four to six months.

Starting on page 142 are a few favorites. But first, let's understand some important African violet terms and definitions.

Episcias have colorful, hairy foliage that can show white, cream, or pink colors.

Try These
A Primer on African Violets

As an amateur African violet collector, or a hobbyist with one or two plants, it can be confusing to read catalogs and figure out exactly what is being described. Whether you are looking to order more African violets, or just want to find out more about the plants you have, here are some helpful African violet terms, and their definitions.

Bloom Type:

Single: Flower has one layer of petals, i.e., five petals in all.

Double: Flower with at least two layers of petals.

Semi-Double: Flower with more petals than a single, but not enough to be called a double.

Star: Flower on which the petals are of equal size.

Wasp: Flower that is a single, but on which the top two, smaller petals curl back.

Frilled: Flower has a wavy appearance.

Bloom Pattern:

Bicolor: Flower exhibits two colors.

Edged: Flower with an edge that differs in color from the rest of the flower.

Fantasy: Flower is dotted or splashed with either a different color or a different shade of the same color.

Pinwheel: Flower has bicolor rays which emanate from the center of the flower and continue to the edge of the petals. The effect gives the flower a pinwheel appearance.

Leaf Type:

Plain: Leaf has no remarkable characteristics.

Pointed: Leaf is pointed at the end. Variations of a pointed leaf include heart-shaped leaves and narrow leaves.

Quilted: Leaf on which the areas between the veins are raised, giving the leaf a puffy, distinctively quilted look.

Red Reverse: Leaf has a reddish-purple underside.

Round: Leaf is nearly circular in shape.

Ruffled: Leaf has a ruffled edge. A tightly ruffled edge is often called curly or lacy. A loosely ruffled edge is often called undulate or wavy.

Serrated: Leaf has a serrated or saw-toothed edge.

Spooned: The edges of the leaf turn up slightly to give the leaf a cupped or a "spooned" appearance.

Variegated: Leaf which exhibits two distinct colors (e.g., green and white) or two distinct tones of the same color (e.g., green and light green).

Plant Type:

Miniature: An African violet that is typically 4 to 6 inches in diameter and is normally grown in a 2-inch pot.

Super-miniature: Plant that is typically 3 to 4 inches in diameter and is grown in a 1-inch pot.

Micro-miniature: The smallest African violet with a diameter that is typically 2 inches or less.

Semi-miniature: Measures 6 to 8 inches in diameter and typically grown in a 3-inch pot.

Standard: An African violet that is single-crowned and has a diameter of 8 inches or more. In terms of size, standard African violets are classified as either small, medium, large or extra large. They normally grow in pots 4 inches or larger.

Trailer: An African violet which has more than one crown.

The "typical" African violet has been bred for long bloom time.

Cape primroses root from cuttings.

African violets (*Saintpaulia* spp.)

The originals, natives of central Africa, all have single blue, purple, or white flowers but hybrids are now available with single or double blooms in every color and combination imaginable. Some even have variegated leaves. Given enough light, these are truly everblooming.

How to grow: African violets thrive in normal house temperatures but will stop blooming when temperatures go above 85°F. If the temperature dips below 60°F, they will seem to grow fur coats, with the leaves becoming hairy and dull. Numerous gardening books recommend growing these plants in filtered light but I've seen many violets fail because they receive too little light.

If your African violet's leaves reach up on long stems, the plant needs more light. A nice flat rosette is the goal. Water your plants with warm water when the surface of the soil is dry. Cold water will spot the leaves even if the water doesn't touch them.

Cape primrose (*Streptocarpus* spp.)

As the name implies, these plants are natives of South Africa. There are stemmed species and rosette types. The stemmed ones are often sold as "dancing ladies," so named for their delicate blue or

Don't overlook the foliage of cape primroses!

purple flowers that float on long stems above the leaves. The other type of streptocarpus has long textured leaves and large bell-like flowers in red, pink, white, or purple, many with striped throats or netted petals.

How to grow: Cape primroses like cooler temperatures than violets but the newer hybrids can take more heat than than the original species. They like air movement and are happy on a sheltered porch in summer. Provide bright light but protect these plants from hot sun because the long leaves are susceptible to sunscorch. Let the pot dry out almost to the wilting point before watering thoroughly.

Chocolate soldier (*Episcia* spp.)

Also called flame violet, chocolate soldier is the name of one brown-leafed hybrid. These are low-growing, fibrous-rooted plants with handsomely patterned leaves in shades of green, pink, orange, cream, yellow and silver. The small flat-faced flowers may be red, orange, yellow, pink, white, or bicolored. Episcias send out long stems from the leaf axils with new plantlets on the ends, called stolons. If these are cut off, it encourages more bloom.

How to grow: If you have an area of your home that's extra warm, that's the site for your episcias. These delicate plants will die at temperatures of 55°F or lower. The brighter the light, short of scorching the leaves, the more bloom. If the edges of the leaves dry, set the plant on a tray filled with pebbles or perlite, and pour water into the bottom to cover the rocks. As the water evaporates, it humidifies the air around the plant. You can easily start new plants from the stolons. Do this once a year or so, as unused fertilizer salts collect on the lower stem and can kill the plant.

Gloxinia (*Sinningia* spp.)

The huge bell-flowered florist gloxinias are only the tip of the iceberg in this extensive group. There are compact types more suitable for windowsills, "slipper-flowered" species, which have a different flower shape, and tiny "minisins," which are smaller. In addition there are stemmed types such as *S. cardinalis*, with its velvety heart-shaped leaves and brilliant red tube flowers. These are all tuberous plants from Brazil.

How to grow: Gloxinias grow from tubers that are usually available from bulb suppliers in fall or spring. Plant them hollow side up, just even with the soil surface. Take care in watering until they begin to grow because water that pools in the bulb's depression may cause rot.

Gloxinias require more light than true African violets. Morning sun or a spot close to fluorescent tubes will keep them compact. If you purchase a budded plant, the buds may not open — a problem called bud blast. The extreme change in humidity the plant experiences when it moves between the greenhouse and your home causes this. A pebble tray will help and the next round of bloom will adjust to your conditions. Water when the surface of the soil is dry. When there is no new growth, reduce watering. In the late winter or spring, the plant will usually resprout but if it bloomed in late summer or fall, it may stay dormant until the following spring.

Gloxinias need a dormant period.

Gloxinias bloom but then go dormant.

Lipstick vines (Aeschynanthus *spp.) have vivid flowers.*

Lipstick vine (*Aeschynanthus* spp.)

The familiar lipstick vine with its red flowers protruding from a solid calyx tube is only one of a diverse genus. It tends to grow very large but there are smaller basket varieties and an upright one called *A. hildebrandii* for pots. Flowers come in red, yellow, orange, and combinations of these colors. Some species flower at the tips but others flower all along the stem.

How to grow: These plants require some sunlight to bloom well and are susceptible to leaf drop if overwatered. Let the soil partially dry out between thorough waterings. Cut plant back to the pot's edge after blooming to force new growth from the base.

Resurrection plant (*Achimenes* spp.)

Also known as nut orchid, cupid's bower, and hot water plant, achimenes will grow from 6 to 18 inches tall, depending on the variety. The leaves are usually dark green and oval shaped with toothed edges, although some leaves have red undersides. A long flower tube protrudes from the leafy calyx and five petals lie horizontally. The lobes may be from ½ to 3 inches across in white, purple, pink, red, or yellow. There are double hybrids with a cluster of extra petals in the throat.

How to grow: Native to Central America, these plants grow from rhizomes that are readily available from mailorder sources in the spring. Plant sprouted rhizomes about half an inch deep. You can plant up to 5 rhizomes in a 4-inch pot, and 10 to 12 in a 6-inch basket. If the rhizomes are not already sprouted, either leave them in the package until they start growth or bury them in a pot of damp vermiculite. I've found that planting dormant rhizomes in soil tends to make them rot. Once green shoots appear, gently pull up the rhizomes and replant them in a good potting mix.

Keep these plants in bright light, protected from midday sun, and keep the soil moist. Snipping off the top half of the plant when the plant is 6 inches tall will result in branching and a more compact plant. The trimmings root easily and will bloom with the parent.

Allowing the plant to dry out will trigger dormancy and the production of rhizomes for the next season. Yellowing lower leaves indicate dormancy and the plant should be allowed to dry out completely between waterings. New rhizomes will form in the soil at a ratio of perhaps 10 to one and will sprout again after four months' dormancy.

Uncommon favorites

Collecting these elegant plants can be an engrossing hobby. Below are a few of the more uncommon types you may want to investigate, as well.

Alsobia 'Cygnet'

Fibrous rooted. This plant has blue-green foliage and fringed white flowers spotted with red. It may be a basket or pot plant if you take off the stolons.

Alsobia 'Cygnet' is a relative of Episcia.

Chirita sinensis *'Hisako' has elegant foliage.*

Chirita sinensis 'Hisako'

Fibrous-rooted rosette plant with silver and green variegated leaves. Occasionally bears mauve blossoms but it is grown mostly for foliage.

Kohlerias have foxglove-like flowers.

Guppy plant (Nematanthus spp.)

Most of these are fibrous-rooted basket plants with shiny green leaves and tiny pouched flowers in red, orange or yellow. The species *N. tropicana* with its striped flowers may be grown as a pot plant or outdoor summer bedding plant.

Kohleria spp.

These rhizomatous plants tend to grow tall but you can cut the tips with buds off and root them under clear plastic. They will continue to bloom. The flat-faced flowers are heavily spotted on red, pink, or yellow backgrounds.

African violet leaves root well. Although leaves will root in water, try to keep the stems from touching the bottom of the glass. Because these leaves root so readily, many people prefer to start them in soil or wet sand.

"Guppy" plants (Nematanthus spp.) have puffy flowers.

W I N T E R
ENTERTAINING

Other than the holidays, folks in winter just seem to hole up, hibernate and wait until spring to gather again. Not necessary! In fact, now it's more important than ever to get together and socialize. That's why we're presenting you with these five complete menus, and ideas for how and when to use them. They won't work you to the bone. But the tastes and beauty of the dishes you prepare will make it seem like they did.

Facing page: Chocolate Amaretto Dipping Sauce, page 170

HOLIDAY BRUNCH

You don't have to get up at dawn to make a special brunch to celebrate a holiday. Prepare everything the day ahead and enjoy the season. There's no need to get stressed out. These ideas make daytime entertaining easy!

Menu

~ Orange Pecan Stuffed French Toast
~ Orange Pecan Maple Syrup
~ Crunchy Turkey Patties
~ Winter Fruit Salad
~ Orange Balsamic Vinaigrette

Entertains 8

ORANGE PECAN STUFFED FRENCH TOAST

This fancy stuffed French toast is perfect for any celebration. You can also celebrate how easy it is to make!

1	(8-oz.) pkg. cream cheese
⅓	cup sugar
⅓	cup chopped toasted pecans*
1	tablespoon grated orange peel
16	(1-inch) slices French bread
4	eggs, beaten
¼	cup milk
1	teaspoon vanilla
¼	cup (½ stick) butter

1 In medium bowl, blend cream cheese, sugar, pecans and orange peel.

2 Cut bread horizontally ⅔ of the way through middle of each slice to form a pocket. Place spoonful of cream cheese mixture into each pocket; press to close.

3 In another medium bowl, combine eggs, milk and vanilla. Dip each bread slice into egg mixture.

4 In large saucepan, heat 2 tablespoons of the butter over medium heat until melted. Add 8 slices of the bread; cook about 2 minutes per side or until golden. Repeat with remaining butter and bread.

5 Serve hot with plain syrup or *Orange Pecan Maple Syrup* (page 151).

8 Servings.
Preparation time: 20 minutes.
Ready to serve: 30 minutes.
Per Serving: 340 calories, 225 g fat (11 g saturated fat), 155 mg cholesterol, 295 mg sodium, 15 g fiber.

Menu Tip

• To toast pecans, spread on baking sheet; bake at 375°F 5 minutes or until lightly browned. Cool.

Before the Event

The filling for the French toast can be mixed a day ahead and the bread can be stuffed, covered with plastic wrap and refrigerated until ready to cook.

ORANGE PECAN MAPLE SYRUP

Real maple syrup is an indulgence, but worth it. It also tastes better when heated, compared to artificial syrups.

2   cups maple syrup
¼   cup chopped toasted pecans*
2   tablespoons grated orange peel

1 In medium saucepan, combine syrup, pecans and orange peel; warm over low heat.

8 Servings.
Preparation time: 15 minutes.
Ready to serve: 20 minutes.
Per Serving: 230 calories, 25 g fat (0 g saturated fat), 0 mg cholesterol, 10 mg sodium, 0 g fiber.

Menu Tip
- To toast pecans, spread on baking sheet; bake at 375°F for 5 minutes or until lightly browned. Cool.

Before the Event
Prepare the *Orange Pecan Maple Syrup* the day before and store in the refrigerator until you're ready to warm it for serving.

CRUNCHY TURKEY PATTIES

These patties are delicious but surprisingly lean. They taste superb on their own and even better when splashed with a little syrup.

1   lb. lean ground turkey breast
1   egg
1   (8-oz.) can water chestnuts, drained, chopped
¼   cup chopped green onions
1   cup fresh bread crumbs
½   teaspoon salt
½   teaspoon freshly ground pepper

1 Heat oven to 400°F.

2 In large bowl, combine turkey, egg, water chestnuts, green onions, bread crumbs, salt and pepper; blend thoroughly. Form turkey mixture into 8 (1-inch-thick) patties.

3 Spray baking sheet with nonstick cooking spray. Arrange patties on baking sheet. Bake 15 minutes or until patties are no longer pink inside.

8 Servings.
Preparation time: 15 minutes.
Ready to serve: 30 minutes.
Per serving: 110 calories, 25 g fat (1 g saturated fat), 60 mg cholesterol, 215 mg sodium, 1 g fiber.

Before the Event

Make *Crunchy Turkey Patties* a day ahead, then cook just before serving.

WINTER FRUIT SALAD

You don't have to wait for summer to enjoy fresh fruit. The fruits in this salad are at their best when it's winter almost everywhere else.

2   medium pink grapefruit, peeled, sectioned
1   medium orange, peeled, sectioned
2   medium red pears, cored, sliced
1   cup seedless red grapes
8   cups mixed greens

1 Arrange grapefruit, orange, pear slices and grapes over greens on large serving platter; drizzle with *Orange Balsamic Vinaigrette* (page 155) before serving.

8 Servings.
Preparation time: 25 minutes.
Ready to serve: 25 minutes.
Per serving: 75 calories, 0.5 g fat (0 g saturated fat), 0 mg cholesterol, 15 mg sodium, 3 g dietary fiber.

Menu Tip

• To easily section the citrus fruit in *Winter Fruit Salad*, start by peeling the fruit with a paring knife to remove all the white pith. With the sections exposed, place a sharp paring knife on one side of the section membrane and cut down, then cut down on the other side and remove the section. Continue around the fruit.

Before the Event

Section fruit a day ahead.

ORANGE BALSAMIC VINAIGRETTE

This light citrus dressing is perfect for *Winter Fruit Salad* (page 154). In this recipe you may want to try white balsamic vinegar. It is especially useful when you don't want to darken a vinaigrette or sauce.

¼ cup olive oil
¼ cup orange juice
3 tablespoons balsamic vinegar
1 tablespoon honey
⅛ teaspoon salt
⅛ teaspoon freshly ground pepper

1 In small bowl, combine oil, orange juice, vinegar, honey, salt and pepper until blended. Drizzle over *Winter Fruit Salad.*

Serves 8
Preparation time: 10 minutes.
Ready to serve: 10 minutes.
Per serving: 70 calories, 65 g fat (1 g saturated fat), 0 mg cholesterol, 35 mg sodium, 0 g fiber.

Before the Event
You can make *Orange Balsamic Vinaigrette* a day ahead.

CHINESE NEW YEAR

Whether it's the Chinese year of the dog or the dragon, this is a great way to treat friends to a terrific meal with an Asian accent. Get together a little early, get all hands involved, and make the preparation part of the party! Everybody loves to keep busy.

Menu

~ Lamb with Colorful Peppers
~ Chinese Noodle Pancake
~ Crab Rangoon in Wonton Baskets
~ Five-Spice Nuts
~ Sesame Cookies

Entertains 4

LAMB WITH COLORFUL PEPPERS

Chili oil adds a bite of heat to this lamb dish. The oil is available in the international aisle of many grocery stores, or in Asian markets.

2   tablespoons chili oil
1   tablespoon minced fresh ginger
1   lb. boneless leg of lamb, cut into thin strips
2   bell peppers (orange, red or yellow), cut into thin strips
8   oz. mushrooms, sliced
1   bunch green onions, chopped
⅓   cup oyster sauce

1 In wok, heat oil over high heat until hot. Add ginger; stir-fry about 30 seconds. Add lamb; stir-fry until golden brown. Remove lamb from wok; set aside.

2 Add bell peppers, mushrooms and green onions to wok; stir-fry about 1 minute or until warmed through but still crispy.

3 Return lamb to wok; stir in oyster sauce. Cook about 1 minute or until warmed through.

4 Servings.
Preparation time: 20 minutes.
Ready to serve: 30 minutes.
Per serving: 300 calories, 15 g fat (4 g saturated fat), 80 mg cholesterol, 970 mg sodium, 25 g fiber.

Before the Event
Chop all the ingredients for the stir-fry earlier in the day. Cover and refrigerate until you are ready to cook.

CHINESE NOODLE PANCAKE

With its crunchy crust and soft middle, this pancake comes out more like hash browns made

with noodles.

8   oz. Chinese noodles or angel hair pasta
4   green onions, finely chopped
2   tablespoons vegetable oil

1 Cook noodles in large pot of boiling water about 2 minutes; drain.

2 In medium bowl, toss cooked noodles with green onions.

3 In medium skillet, heat oil over medium-high heat until hot. Add pasta; press mixture into a pancake. Reduce heat to medium. Cook about 5 minutes or until golden brown crust forms. Flip pancake. Add more oil if necessary; continue to cook an additional 5 minutes or until crust forms. Place pancake on platter; top with Lamb with Colorful Peppers (page 158).

4 Servings.
Preparation time: 10 minutes.
Ready to serve: 10 minutes.
Per serving: 195 calories, 7 g fat (1 g saturated fat), 0 mg cholesterol, 5 mg sodium, 1 g fiber.

Before the Event

Cook noodles earlier in the day, then rinse with cold water and refrigerate until you're ready to make the pancakes.

CRAB RANGOON IN WONTON BASKETS

In restaurants, the crab mixture is stuffed in a wonton and deep-fat fried. This presentation is easier to prepare, better for you, and every bit as tasty.

24	wonton wrappers squares, cut into circles with a cookie cutter
1	tablespoon olive oil
12	oz. crabmeat
½	cup lightly toasted almonds*
1	(8-oz.) pkg. cream cheese
3	green onions, minced
½	teaspoon salt
¼	teaspoon freshly ground pepper, plus more to taste

1 Heat oven to 350°F.

2 Coat miniature muffin pans with nonstick cooking spray. Press a wonton circle into each muffin cup. Lightly coat circles with olive oil; bake 7 to 10 minutes or until lightly brown. Remove from oven to cool.

3 Meanwhile, in medium bowl, combine crab, almonds, cream cheese, green onions, salt and pepper. Fill cooled wonton cups with crab mixture.

4 Servings.
Preparation time: 20 minutes.
Ready to serve: 20 minutes.
Per serving: 510 calories, 345 g fat (14 g saturated fat), 165 mg cholesterol, 720 mg sodium, 3 g fiber.

Menu Tip

- To toast almonds, place on baking sheet; bake at 375°F for about 4 minutes or until light golden brown.

Before the Event

Make the crab mixture a day ahead, cover and refrigerate. You can also make the wonton cups ahead, but store in an airtight container at room temperature.

FIVE-SPICE NUTS

Five-spice powder is a mixture of ground cinnamon, anise, ginger, allspice and cloves. If

it's not available at your local grocery, try an Asian market.

2   tablespoons sugar
1   teaspoon five-spice powder
1   cup dry-roasted peanuts
2   tablespoons sesame oil

1 Heat oven to 325°F.

2 In small bowl, combine sugar, five-spice powder and peanuts. Drizzle oil over nuts; toss to coat.

3 Spread peanuts on large baking sheet. Bake 15 minutes or until golden brown and fragrant, stirring once.

4 Servings.
Preparation time: 5 minutes.
Ready to serve: 20 minutes.
Per serving: 300 calories, 25 g fat (35 g saturated fat), 0 mg cholesterol, 3 mg sodium, 35 g fiber.

Before the Event

Make *Five-Spice Nuts* ahead and store in an airtight container at room temperature.

Sesame Cookies

Sesame seeds give these simple sugar cookies a decidedly Chinese twist.

2 cups all-purpose flour
1 cup sugar
1 teaspoon baking powder
½ cup shortening
2 eggs
½ to ¾ cup sesame seeds

1 Heat oven to 325°F.

2 In medium bowl, mix flour, sugar and baking powder. Add shortening and eggs; knead dough about 2 minutes or until completely blended.

3 Place dough on parchment paper. Use paper to help roll a long log of dough, about 2 inches in diameter. Cut log into ¼-inch-thick rounds.

4 Press each side of each round into sesame seeds to coat; place on ungreased baking sheets. Bake 15 to 20 minutes or until golden. Remove cookies from pan immediately.

Makes 30 cookies.
Preparation time: 15 minutes.
Ready to serve: 30 minutes.
Per cookie: 100 calories, 5 g fat (1 g saturated fat), 15 mg cholesterol, 20 mg sodium, 0.5 g fiber.

Menu Tip
- Keep sesame seeds for *Sesame Cookies* in the freezer. They have a high fat content and can go rancid quickly at room temperature.

Before the Event
Sesame Cookies can be made ahead and stored in an airtight container at room temperature.

ROMANTIC WINTER DINNER

Turn down the lights, turn on the soft music and light the candles. This elegant dinner for two makes for a cozy and private evening that lets you celebrate both the season and each other.

Menu

~ Puff Pastry Hearts
~ Sautéed Rosemary Veal Chops
~ Red Grape Sauce
~ Jasmine Coconut Rice
~ Chocolate Amaretto Dipping
  Sauce

Entertains 2

PUFF PASTRY HEARTS

These heart-shaped pastries can be assembled and cut ahead of time, but they are at their

mouth-watering best served hot from the oven.

1   tablespoon prepared mustard
½   sheet puff pastry, thawed
3   thin slices honey baked ham
1   oz. fresh basil or baby spinach leaves, stems
     removed
3   thin (5x3-inch) slices Swiss cheese

1 Heat oven to 425°F. Line baking sheet with parchment paper.

2 Spread mustard over thawed pastry. Top mustard with ham, basil and Swiss cheese.

3 Roll short side of dough up, continuing until roll reaches middle of dough. Roll other side until both rolls meet in the middle. Turn roll on its side; press into oval heart shape.

4 Cut rolled dough into about 10 (½-inch) slices using sawing motion with bread knife.

5 Bake slices on baking sheet about 15 minutes or until golden.

2 Servings.
Preparation time: 15 minutes.
Ready to serve: 30 minutes.
Per serving: 310 calories, 215 g fat (10 g saturated fat), 50 mg cholesterol, 620 mg sodium, 1 g fiber.

Menu Tip

- For the best *Puff Pastry Hearts*, keep puff pastry as cold as possible, then put it into a very hot oven.

Before the Event

Puff Pastry Hearts can be assembled, sliced and placed on a baking sheet. Then cover with plastic wrap and refrigerate until you're ready to bake.

Sauteed Rosemary Veal Chops

Veal is for special occasions. This simple presentation showcases the meat's delicate flavor.

2   loin veal chops, about 1 inch thick
½   teaspoon dried crushed rosemary
½   teaspoon salt
¼   teaspoon freshly ground pepper
½   tablespoon butter
1   recipe Red Grape Sauce (page 168)

1 Season chops with rosemary, salt and pepper.

2 In medium skillet, heat butter over medium-high heat until melted. Add chops to skillet; cook 3 minutes, then turn and reduce heat to medium. Continue to cook about 5 minutes.

3 Remove chops to platter; tent with aluminum foil to keep warm while making Red Grape Sauce in same skillet.

2 Servings.
Preparation time: 5 minutes.
Ready to serve: 15 minutes.
Per serving: 335 calories, 20 g fat (11 g saturated fat), 130 mg cholesterol, 755 mg sodium, 1 g fiber.

Before the Event
Season the chops earlier in the day and refrigerate until ready to serve.

RED GRAPE SAUCE

Sherry vinegar adds a distinct flavor and richness to this simply delicious sauce. The red grapes give it a beautiful blush hue. Try this sauce with chicken and pork, as well as *Sautéed Rosemary Veal Chops* (page 167).

1   cup red grapes, halved
3   tablespoons sherry vinegar
2   tablespoons butter
1   teaspoon sugar

1 In medium skillet, combine grapes, vinegar, butter and sugar; cook over medium heat, stirring frequently, about 3 minutes or until grapes are hot and juices are bubbling. Serve over Sautéed Rosemary Veal Chops.

2 Servings.
Preparation time: 5 minutes.
Ready to serve: 8 minutes.
Per serving: 170 calories, 12 g fat (7.5 g saturated fat), 30 mg cholesterol, 75 mg sodium, 1 g fiber.

Before the Event
Slice grapes earlier in the day.

JASMINE COCONUT RICE

This rice has the heavenly aroma of the night-blooming flower that shares its name. On a practical note, it cooks very quickly.

1 tablespoon butter
1 cup jasmine rice
¼ cup flaked sweetened coconut
1½ cups reduced-sodium chicken broth

1 In medium skillet, heat butter over medium heat until melted. Add rice and coconut; cook about 1 minute, stirring constantly.

2 Add chicken broth; bring to a boil. Cover; reduce heat to low. Cook about 15 minutes or until liquid is absorbed and rice is tender.

2 Servings.
Preparation time: 5 minutes.
Ready to serve: 15 minutes.
Per serving: 495 calories, 11 g fat (7 g saturated fat), 15 mg cholesterol, 425 mg sodium, 15 g fiber.

Before the Event

Prepare rice earlier in the day, then microwave on High for 1 minute or until warmed through.

CHOCOLATE AMARETTO DIPPING SAUCE

This dipping sauce tastes so decadent that it's hard to believe how simple it is to make.

Serve with slices of fresh fruit (such as pears, pineapple or strawberries) or cubes of angel food cake.

1	cup cream
6	oz. semisweet chocolate, chopped or chips
1	pasteurized egg
2	tablespoons almond liqueur or 1 teaspoon almond extract

1 In small pan, heat cream to a simmer.

2 In blender, combine cream, chocolate, egg and liqueur; whip until smooth. Pour mixture into individual decorative bowls surrounded by fruit for dipping.

2 Servings.
Preparation time: 5 minutes.
Ready to serve: 15 minutes.
Per serving: 835 calories, 65 g fat (40 g saturated fat), 240 mg cholesterol, 80 mg sodium, 5 g fiber.

Before the Event

Make *Chocolate Amaretto Dipping Sauce* a day ahead and pour into a wine glass. It will set up and become mousse!

FIRESIDE AFTERNOON TEA

Light the fire and get out your best china teacups. This delightful little menu will warm up any chilly afternoon, and serve as the backdrop for a relaxing and elegant get-together to be remembered.

Menu

~ Herbed Triangles
~ Stilton Walnut Fingers
~ Coconut Macaroons
~ Scones
~ Devonshire Cream

Entertains 12

HERBED TRIANGLES

These triangles offer a lovely and fresh taste. But be careful, they can be addictive!

⅓   cup finely chopped green onions
⅓   cup minced fresh parsley
⅓   cup minced fresh dill
12 thin slices white or wheat bread, crusts removed
½   cup (1 stick) unsalted butter, softened

1 In medium bowl, combine green onions, parsley and dill. Place mixture on sheet of parchment paper.

2 Spread each bread slice evenly with butter; cut into triangles. Press buttered side of triangle into herb mixture.

12 Servings.
Preparation time: 20 minutes.
Ready to serve: 20 minutes.
Per serving: 100 calories, 8 g fat (5 g saturated fat), 20 mg cholesterol, 70 mg sodium, 0.5 g fiber.

Menu Tip

- All the recipes in this menu deserve a cup of tea! Here are some suggestions for making a good pot of tea: Warm the teapot by rinsing it with boiling water. Bring freshly drawn water to a boil. Take teapot to the kettle and pour the boiling water. Use 1¼ pints boiling water to each ounce of tea. Stir mixture well, replace lid and allow tea to brew 5 minutes. Pour into warm cups; add milk and sugar to taste. For a golden sheen, brush each *Scone* (page 178) with 1 beaten egg and sprinkle with coarse sugar.

Before the Event

Make *Herbed Triangles* earlier in the day, cover with plastic wrap and refrigerate to keep moist.

Stilton Walnut Fingers

The English call rectangles of toast "fingers." Stilton is a specific type of English blue cheese, but you can use any type of blue cheese in this recipe.

Bread

10 slices raisin bread, crusts removed

Cheese

4 oz. Stilton cheese
1 (8-oz.) pkg. cream cheese, softened
1 tablespoon Port wine (optional)

Garnish

30 walnuts, toasted*
15 red grapes, halved

1 Cut each bread slice into 3 "fingers," then toast.

2 Meanwhile, in medium bowl, combine Stilton, cream cheese and Port into smooth mixture. Spread heaping teaspoon of cheese mixture evenly onto each toast finger.

3 Garnish each with a walnut and a grape half.

12 Servings.
Preparation time: 20 minutes.
Ready to serve: 20 minutes.
Per serving: 185 calories, 13 g fat (65 g saturated fat), 30 mg cholesterol, 255 mg sodium, 1 g fiber.

Menu Tip

- To toast walnuts, spread on baking sheet; bake at 375°F 7 to 10 minutes or until lightly browned. Cool.

Before the Event

Make the Stilton mixture a day ahead and refrigerate. Toast bread "fingers" on a baking sheet at 350°F for 15 minutes, turning once. When cool, place in a large resealable plastic bag until ready to use.

COCONUT MACAROONS

If you love coconut, you will love these cookies. And they are *so* easy to make.

⅓ cup sweetened condensed milk
1   egg white
1   teaspoon almond extract
⅛ teaspoon salt
3   cups shredded sweetened coconut

1 Heat oven to 375°F. Line baking sheet with parchment paper.

2 In medium bowl, combine sweetened condensed milk, egg white, almond extract, salt and coconut.

3 Drop dough by tablespoonfuls onto baking sheet. Bake 16 to 20 minutes or until golden. Remove cookies to wire rack to cool.

12 Servings.
Preparation time: 20 minutes.
Ready to serve: 30 minutes.
Per serving: 175 calories, 10 g fat (8 g saturated fat), 5 mg cholesterol, 110 mg sodium, 1 g fiber.

Before the Event

Make *Coconut Macaroons* ahead and store in an airtight container.

Scones

Even novice bakers can make first-rate scones. They are truly simple and delicious. Unsalted butter is the key ingredient; it adds to the sweet taste.

2½ cups all-purpose flour
¼   cup sugar
1   tablespoon baking powder
½   teaspoon salt
½   cup (1 stick) unsalted butter, cut into pieces
1   cup milk

1 Heat oven to 425°F.

2 In medium bowl, mix flour, sugar, baking powder and salt.

3 Cut in butter until mixture resembles coarse oatmeal. Add milk; blend to form soft dough.

4 Turn dough onto floured board; knead lightly.

5 Divide dough in half; pat each half into ½-inch-thick round. Cut each round into 8 wedges. Arrange wedges 1 inch apart on ungreased baking sheet. Bake 10 to 15 minutes or until golden brown.

Makes 16 scones.
Preparation time: 20 minutes.
Ready to serve: 30 minutes.
Per serving: 140 calories, 6 g fat (4 g saturated fat), 15 mg cholesterol, 170 mg sodium. 0.5 g fiber.

Before the Event
Prepare and cut scone dough ahead of time, then refrigerate or freeze until ready to bake.

DEVONSHIRE CREAM

Rich and tangy Devonshire cream is a must at any tea to serve with *Scones* (page 178). It

is difficult to get the real thing outside of England, but this recipe is just as good.

3   tablespoons powdered sugar
¾   cup sour cream
¾   cup heavy cream, whipped

1 In medium bowl, fold powdered sugar and sour cream into whipped cream.

12 Servings.
Preparation time: 5 minutes.
Ready to serve: 5 minutes.
Per Serving: 80 calories, 75 g fat (45 g saturated fat), 25 mg cholesterol, 10 mg sodium, 0 g fiber.

Before the Event

Prepare *Devonshire Cream* a day ahead and refrigerate in a covered, non-aluminum container until ready to use.

Apres Skating Party

Whether you skate, ski, hike, ride a sled or just shovel snow, this is an appealing menu after (après) any chilly outdoor activity. Even if you don't go outside, these ideas will warm you on even the coldest day.

Menu

~ Tomato Goat Cheese Gratin with Bread Rounds
~ Potato Blue Cheese Soup
~ French Onion Soup
~ Russian Tea
~ Turtle Tart

Entertains 8

Tomato Goat Cheese Gratin with Bread Rounds

Have you noticed the explosion of flavored canned tomatoes? Roasted garlic tomatoes here

add a wealth of wonderful flavor without adding work.

2 (14.5-oz.) cans diced roasted garlic tomatoes
1 tablespoon pesto
2 (4-oz.) pkg. goat cheese, cut into ⅓-inch
   slices
2 tablespoons chopped fresh basil
1 French baguette, sliced into ¼-inch-thick
   rounds

1 In large skillet, heat tomatoes and pesto over medium-high heat about 2 minutes or until juices are reduced and sauce has thickened.

2 Heat oven to 375°F.

3 Pour tomato mixture into shallow casserole; top with cheese slices. Bake about 10 minutes or until cheese has melted. Sprinkle with basil. Serve warm with baguette rounds.

8 Servings.
Preparation time: 5 minutes.
Ready to serve: 15 minutes.
Per Serving: 195 calories, 8.5 g total fat (5 g saturated fat), 25 mg cholesterol, 560 mg sodium, 2 g fiber.

Before the Event

Prepare and assemble tomatoes a day ahead, then heat at the last minute.

POTATO BLUE CHEESE SOUP

Add blue cheese to turn ordinary potato soup into something extraordinary.

1   tablespoon unsalted butter
1   medium onion, thinly sliced
1   small garlic clove, minced
4   medium potatoes, peeled, cubed
4   cups reduced-sodium chicken broth
2   cups half-and-half
1   cup (4 oz.) crumbled blue cheese
⅛   teaspoon salt
⅛   teaspoon freshly ground pepper

1 In large saucepan, heat butter over medium-high heat until melted. Add onion; cook about 5 minutes or until soft but not brown. Add garlic; cook an additional minute.

2 Add potatoes to saucepan; cook 5 minutes. Add broth; bring to a boil. Reduce heat. Cover; simmer about 20 minutes or until potatoes are tender.

3 Add half-and-half; stir in ½ cup of the blue cheese. Season with salt and pepper. Garnish with any remaining cheese.

8 Servings.
Preparation time: 10 minutes.
Ready to serve: 30 minutes.
Per Serving: 230 calories, 14 g total fat (8.5 g saturated fat), 40 mg cholesterol, 540 mg sodium, 15 g fiber.

Before the Event

Make *Potato Blue Cheese Soup* a day ahead.

FRENCH ONION SOUP

The perfect soup to serve in front of the fire on any winter evening.

Caramelized Onions
2   tablespoons butter
6   cups sliced yellow onions

Soup
1   tablespoon all-purpose flour
6   cups beef broth
½   cup red wine (optional)
1   French baguette, cut into ½-inch-thick slices, toasted
8   oz. grated Swiss cheese

1 In large skillet, melt butter. Add onions; cook slowly over low heat, stirring occasionally, until soft and golden, about 1 hour. Cool and refrigerate or freeze until ready to use.

2 Place onions in large soup pot; sprinkle with flour. Cook about 1 minute; add broth and red wine. Cook 20 minutes to allow flavors to blend.

3 Heat broiler. Place bread slices on aluminum foil-lined broiler pan. Sprinkle Swiss cheese over bread; broil about 1 minute or until cheese is melted and bubbling.

4 Serve soup with the Swiss toast rounds.

8 Servings.
Preparation time: 5 minutes.
Ready to serve: 25 minutes.
Per Serving: 265 calories, 115 g total fat (7 g saturated fat), 35 mg cholesterol, 1040 mg sodium, 25 g fiber.

Menu Tip

- Here's how to make a quick version of the caramelized onions: Place 6 cups thinly sliced yellow onions in a microwave-safe bowl with 2 tablespoons butter. Cover the bowl with parchment paper. Microwave on High 15 minutes, stirring once. The microwave can also pre-cook potatoes to speed up the *Potato Blue Cheese Soup* (page 184) as well.

Before the Event

Make *French Onion Soup* a day ahead and refrigerate.

RUSSIAN TEA

Traditionally, *Russian Tea* is poured into a tall glass and sweetened with cherry preserves.

Even when served in a mug, it's a warming and sweet treat. Quality tea bags will make

two good pots of tea.

3 black tea bags
6 cups boiling water
1 lemon, thinly sliced
1 cup cherry preserves

1 Steep tea bags in boiling water about 5 minutes. Serve tea with slice of lemon and spoonfuls of cherry preserves to taste.

8 Servings.
Preparation time: 15 minutes.
Ready to serve: 15 minutes.
Per Serving: 100 calories, 0 g total fat (0 g saturated fat), 0 mg cholesterol, 20 mg sodium, 0.5 g fiber.

Before the Event
Steep teas ahead of time and reheat just before serving.

TURTLE TART

Who doesn't love turtle chocolate candies? This delightful tart brings together the chocolate, caramel and nut flavors that make the candy so good.

1	prepared pie shell
12	oz. dark chocolate chips
½	cup cream
2	cups toasted pecans*
1	cup caramel ice cream topping

1 Heat oven to 425°F.

2 Roll dough into 10-inch circle. Press circle into 9-inch tart pan; trim excess dough. Bake 10 minutes or until golden brown.

3 Meanwhile, heat chocolate and cream in microwave on High 1 minute; stir until melted. Spread melted chocolate mixture into bottom of baked tart shell; top with pecans. Chill in freezer until set.

4 Serve tart topped with ice cream topping.

8 Servings.
Preparation time: 15 minutes.
Ready to serve: 30 minutes.
Per Serving: 715 calories, 50 g total fat (20 g saturated fat), 45 mg cholesterol, 230 mg sodium, 5 g fiber.

Menu Tip
- To toast pecans, spread on baking sheet; bake at 375°F for 5 minutes or until lightly browned. Cool.

Before the Event
Make *Turtle Tart* a day ahead, cover and store at room temperature.

INDEX